GOD'S *Favorite* HOUSE

Journal

If You Build It, He Will Come

GOD'S *Favorite* HOUSE

Journal

If You Build It, He Will Come

Includes excerpts from:

Thomas à Kempis • Dietrich Bonhoeffer • Hannah More

Watchman Nee • Phoebe Palmer • Jessie Penn-Lewis

Sadhu Sundar Singh • T. Austin Sparks • Teresa of Ávila

A.W. Tozer • Smith Wigglesworth

TOMMY TENNEY

Fresh Bread

An Imprint of
Destiny Image® **Publishers, Inc.**
P.O. Box 310
Shippensburg, PA 17257-0310

ISBN 0-7684-2107-1

For Worldwide Distribution
Printed in the U.S.A.

This book and all other Destiny Image, Revival Press, MercyPlace, Fresh Bread, and Treasure House books are available at Christian bookstores and distributors worldwide.

For a U.S. bookstore nearest you, call **1-800-722-6774**.
For more information on foreign distributors, call **717-532-3040**.
Or reach us on the Internet: **http://www.reapernet.com**

Introduction

Family photo albums and scrapbooks are precious things. No two are alike. On the surface, these collections of photos, cards, and clippings may not seem very valuable. But we don't cherish them for their physical worth: it's the memories that make them meaningful. My family's pictures and stories may not mean much to you, but they are the world to me. You probably feel the same about your special memories.

That's why I enjoy creating these journals. No matter what I write, no matter how much my encounters with God mean to me, they're still mine, and they'll never have the same value to you. It isn't enough to observe God's relationships with others—you must cultivate a relationship of your own. In these pages, you'll be challenged to focus on God and worship Him like never before—to spend time with Him in His favorite place.

You can turn this journal into a scrapbook of sorts—preserving verbal snapshots of special moments with your heavenly Father. Make it personal—don't be afraid to draw pictures or write poetry. Don't worry about what anyone else might think if they were to see this. You didn't draw or write for them. This is from you, for your Father. Whatever you do, if it comes from a heart of sincere worship, He will treasure it for eternity.

—Tommy Tenney
Author, GodChaser

Helpful Tips for Your Chase

This is the second journal created to help you personalize your chase of the Lord Jesus. If you choose, you may quickly read through this journal in a very short period of time, but you will miss the whole point of the journal. The journal is to be a resource that will help you go deeper in your thoughts and contemplation that were started in the reading of *God's Favorite House*. The author and the publishers want to encourage you to prayerfully meditate on these powerful truths. As you do so, this journal will become a motivational tool that will help move you to new levels of intimacy with the Lord Jesus and enable you to return to those new levels.

To Learn His Presence

It is our hope that this journal will help you live in the presence of the Lord every day. It is not intended to simply add new truth to a bag that is already full; rather, it is our desire that it will bring you to a place of new experiences with God.

But it will require that you spend time thinking about each individual quote. Let them sink into your heart as you contemplate their spiritual meaning, applying them to your life, and ultimately letting them lead you to a quiet place of prayer and communion with your Divine Lover, the Lord Jesus.

Begin Your Journey

Few of us have the opportunity for quiet meditation and personal contemplation every day. Therefore, the pages are not dated. Use this journal when you have the time to give yourself to prayer and meditation. It will not help you if you simply make this experience a part of a daily regimen of religious duty.

To begin the journey, it is imperative that you find a quiet place where you can get alone with your journal, your Bible, and your Lord. Read each quote several times, making sure that you have captured the essence of the writer's thoughts. Do not be content with a casual glance before quickly moving on to the next quote. Allow the Spirit of the Lord to enter your thought processes and bring fresh insight. Let the words become a prayer that is formed on your lips.

The practice of contemplative prayer is certainly a lost art in our Western society. We are used to having our spiritual food gathered, prepared, cooked, and delivered to our table by our favorite preachers of the day. This journal will provide you with an opportunity to break out of this rut.

You might want to talk to your friends about the quote and get their thoughts and reactions. How about memorizing the quote so that you can think on it during the day?

Come back to these words several times. Do not be satisfied with only one look. Often, days down the road, fresh meaning and application will come to you.

Here are a few questions that will help guide you in your search:

1. What is the main focus and intent of the author's words?

2. How does this concept apply to my life?

3. What Scripture verses will lead me into further application of this truth?

4. What circumstances have I gone through that enrich the meaning of these statements?

5. Are there any particular areas of my life that need adjustment so that I can move into a new level of experiencing the power of this truth?

6. What is preventing me right now from experiencing the reality of these powerful insights?

7. How can I form the truths of this quote into a personal prayer to the Lord?

Perhaps a good landmark to begin with would be these words, which Francis de Sales wrote in his *Introduction to the Devout Life*:

"A blind man when in the presence of his prince will preserve a reverential demeanour if told that the king is there, although unable to see him; but practically, what men do not see they easily forget, and so readily lapse into carelessness and irreverence. Just so, my child, we do not see our God, and although faith warns us that He is present, not beholding Him with our mortal eyes, we are too apt to forget Him, and act as though He were afar: for, while knowing perfectly that He is everywhere, if we do not think about it, it is much as though we knew it not. And therefore, before beginning to pray, it is needful always to rouse the soul to a steadfast remembrance and thought of the Presence of God. This is what David meant when he exclaimed, 'If I climb up to Heaven, Thou art there, and if I go down to hell, Thou art there also!" [Ps. 139:8] And in like manner Jacob, who, beholding the ladder which went up to Heaven, cried out, 'Surely the Lord is in this place and I knew it not' [Gen. 28:16] meaning thereby that he had not thought of it; for assuredly he could not fail to know that God was everywhere and in all things. Therefore, when you make ready to pray, you must say with your whole heart, 'God is indeed here' " (70).

GOD'S *Favorite* HOUSE JOURNAL

Day	Date	Time	Location

Passion or Palace?

After this I will return and will rebuild the tabernacle of David, which has fallen down; I will rebuild its ruins, and I will set it up (Acts 15:16 NKJV).

I thought to myself, *I wonder why God wants to rebuild that "house"?*...David's makeshift shelter barely qualifies as a tabernacle when it is compared to the tabernacle of Moses, and certainly when compared to Solomon's temple. It amounted to little more than a tarp stretched over some tent poles to shield the ark from the sun and the elements. Yet God said, "I am going to rebuild that one." Evidently, *what is impressive to God and what is impressive to men* are two different things....For some reason the Christian world has forgotten that God has never been impressed by buildings....Our attachment to steeples and stained glass can get in the way of real worship. If given a choice, God prefers passion over palace!...*We want God encounters but God wants man encounters,* because encounters with His children affect Him. He will "rip veils" and interrupt time to visit with His kids.

(*God's Favorite House*, 4-6)

God doesn't just want visiting hours with His children. He wants full custody.

(*God's Favorite House*, 8)

...He Will Come

Day	Date	Time	Location

The Torn Veil

The tabernacle of Moses and Solomon's temple featured three distinct enclosed areas: the outer court, the Holy Place, and the Holy of Holies. A great veil (a heavy drapery in our modern colloquialism) was stretched across the tabernacle to separate the Holy Place from the Holy of Holies where the ark of the covenant rested....The ark, the mercy seat, and the blue flame of God's presence were always hidden behind the thick fabric of the veil.

God never did like that veil. He had to have it, but He didn't like it. When Jesus died on the cross at Calvary, God was the one who ripped the veil from top to bottom in the temple of Herod in Jerusalem. He ripped it in such a way that it could never be rewoven again. *He hated that veil like a prisoner hates his cell door!* It represented the wall, the dividing line that separated Him from mankind. Until that day on Calvary, God had to hide behind the veil to preserve the life of the fallen humanity that came to worship Him in His holiness.

(God's Favorite House, 8-9)

_____

_____

_____

_____

_____

_____

_____

_____

_____

_____

_____

_____

_____

Unveiled worship creates unhindered view!
(God's Favorite House, 10)

| Day | Date | Time | Location |

God Loves Us for Ourselves

David's tabernacle was the only one of any of these structures that had no veil. This key can begin to unravel one of the most important pieces of the wisdom of the ages: *God really doesn't want to be separated from us.* In fact, He will do everything possible to destroy things that separate and hide Him from us. He hates sin because it separates. God went so far as to rip the "veil" of His Son's flesh on Mount Calvary. At the same time, unseen hands ripped the veil on Mount Zion, as if to say, "I don't ever want this thing rewoven again! I am tired of being separated from My children." *God doesn't just want visiting hours with His children. He wants full custody!* He "has broken down the middle wall of separation" (Eph. 2:14b NKJV).

(*God's Favorite House*, 9)

The living God has been willing to reveal Himself to our seeking hearts. He would have us know and understand that He is all love and that those who trust Him need never know anything but that love....This is the best of good news: God loves us for ourselves. He values our love more than He values galaxies of new created worlds.

(A. W. Tozer, *Whatever Happened to Worship?*, 28-29)

_____

_____

_____

_____

_____

_____

_____

_____

_____

_____

_____

_____

_____

_____

_____

_____

_____

Aiden Wilson Tozer was born April 21, 1897, on a small farm among the spiny ridges of western Pennsylvania. Within a few short years, Tozer would earn the reputation and title of a "20th-century prophet."

Tozer's forte was his prayer life, which often found him walking the aisles of a sanctuary or lying facedown on the floor. He noted, "As a man prays, so is he." To him the worship of God was paramount in his life and ministry. In a small cemetery in Akron, Ohio, his tombstone bears this simple epitaph: "A Man of God."

Some wonder why Tozer's writings are as fresh today as when he was alive. It is because, as one friend commented, "He left the superficial, the obvious and the trivial for others to toss around....[His] books reach deep into the heart."

For almost 50 years, Tozer walked with God. Even though he is gone, he continues to speak, ministering to those who are eager to experience God. As someone put it, "This man makes you want to know and feel God."

Tozer's book, *The Pursuit of God*, has always been a favorite of mine.

Day	Date	Time	Location

Carrying the Flame

*The miracle of "God's favorite house" can be traced to David's desire for God's presence....*His first attempt to bring the ark of the covenant to Jerusalem ended in disaster; it resulted in a complete over-haul of David's methods for "handling the holy." When David and his procession of Levites and worshipers finally reached Jerusalem after a grueling 15-mile journey by foot, David may have been dancing as much out of relief as he was out of joy: "We made it!"

Somewhere in the process of transporting that ark and honor-ing God, *David began to value the things that God values.* On the other hand, his wife *Michal valued dignity over Deity....*

Intimate encounters with God are sometimes embarrassing on the stage of man. The landscape of American Christianity is littered with barren churches who have turned their backs on the intimacy of worship. These are modern-day Michals who also have chosen to value dignity over intimacy with Deity....

David was after that blue flame of God's glory....

We can build nicer buildings, raise up larger choirs, write bet-ter music, and preach greater sermons—we can do everything with more excellence than before. But if we are not carrying the "blue flame," then God isn't pleased....Let's turn up the heat of worship.

(God's Favorite House, 10-11)

The Church's reluctance to pay the seemingly high cost of intimate worship is the root cause of our barrenness.

(God's Favorite House, 18)

Day	Date	Time	Location

We Have Lost the Spirit

Too often we want just enough of God in our place of worship to give us a tingle or make a little chill run up our spines....There has to be more to it than thrills and chills. David wasn't content to have a temporary visitation. He was after more...With very few exceptions, church sanctuaries are the most unused rooms in America and around the world. While steady streams of people flock to 24-hour convenience stores to stock up on passing earthly needs, our churches can barely operate two hours per week because the demand for their "product" is so low....If David looked at his humble tabernacle and said, "Someday I hope to do better," then God answered, "A tent will do, David. Just keep your heart hot!"

We have built beautiful sanctuaries with hardly anyone inside because, if there is no flame, there is nothing to see. There is no *shekinah* glory in our churches because we have lost our ability to *host the Holy Ghost.*

(God's Favorite House, 12-13)

We have lost our spirit of worship and our ability to withdraw inwardly to meet God in adoring silence.

(A. W. Tozer, from *The Knowledge of the Holy*, quoted in *Gems From Tozer*, 12)

Day	Date	Time	Location

Face to Face With God

It is in the darkness with God that we learn His judgments; it is in the glory "within the veil" that we are shown His pattern for our lives. It is after the darkness, and the judgments, and the sprinkled blood, that we go even part of the way up the mount and have that vision of God, where His light streams into our lives, and we eat and drink as in His presence, having fellowship one with another, with the blood of Jesus cleansing from all sin; but *alone* we are called to enter the cloud, and dwell in the devouring fire; alone, and only alone, we enter the secret place of the Most High, and know Him "face to face."

(Jessie Penn-Lewis, *Face To Face*, 43).

I want God to show up in His *shekinah* or tangible glory. Compared to Him, everything and everyone else is reduced to a warm-up act filling time until the Real Thing enters the room. I am afraid that we have built a religion and a lifestyle around the appetizers while completely forgetting the main course!

(*God's Favorite House*, 15)

In the early 1900s, at a time when few women were called to public ministry, **Jessie Penn-Lewis** used her pen and her presence to impact thousands of people for the Kingdom. The 50 or so books and booklets that she wrote have found their way all around the globe.

War on the Saints, published in 1912, was her most recognized work. She was particularly known for her great writings on spiritual warfare, but the message of the Cross was always the heartbeat of her life. Her book *The Magna Carta of Christian Women* stood as a signpost in the swirl of heated debate surrounding women's place in ministry.

No one should forget the key role she played in the Welsh Revival. Evan Roberts joined with Mrs. Penn-Lewis in penning some of her writings on the overcoming life. Roberts said that Jessie Penn-Lewis was a mystic with a Welsh Methodist background who was able to define the inner workings of man's nature.

You may disagree with this somewhat controversial woman, but one thing all will agree on is her personal passion for the presence of God. For 30 years, Jessie Penn-Lewis was the messenger of the Lord and her writings still stand as some of the best works on the power of the overcomer. May the world be graced with more like Jessie Penn-Lewis.

GOD'S *Favorite* HOUSE JOURNAL

Day	Date	Time	Location

Stopping Short of the Glory

We experience a taste or a fleeting hint of God's glory every time we find ourselves in places where what we call "revival" has broken out....

When this happens, we tend to handle the situation much of the time like inexperienced runners in a sprint race. We explode from the blocks in eager pursuit of God's presence and continue at a fast pace until we begin to feel the discomfort of an all-consuming hunt for the trophy of our heart's desire.

Some of us feel our strength failing and our senses becoming dull to things around us as we gasp for breath. With one last burst of desperate energy we stretch forward and lunge toward the line...only to stumble forward and fall several yards *short* of the finish line. By stopping too soon, by failing to press forward all the way through to the finish, *we are racing to false finish lines and fail to seize the prize....*

Too often we stop at false finish lines because our flesh gets excited. We want to interrupt God's revelation of Himself so we can build sand castles in honor of the first premonition of His appearing. We are so busy saying, "It is good we are here," that we don't hear God say, "I want to join you there too."

(God's Favorite House, 15-17)

I'm weary of reading about revival—I must meet the "Reviver."

(*God's Favorite House*, 19)

Day	Date	Time	Location

A Fleeting Fragrance

God is looking for a person, a church, and a city that will hear His gentle knock and open the door for Him. The Scriptures continually picture the Lord knocking on doors in both the Old and New Testaments. We see Him prophetically knocking on the door of His *own* house in the Song of Solomon, seeking the attention of His Beloved, the Church (see Song 5:2)....

The Lover of our souls has persistently knocked at the doors of His House, but we respond exactly like Solomon's bride:

I have taken off my robe—must I put it on again? I have washed my feet—must I soil them again? (Song 5:3 NIV)

God's betrothed Lover and Bride has become too comfortable. She refuses to open the door because it isn't convenient. The cost of intimacy seems too high. The discomfort of it all has bred an apathy that urges us to move too slowly and casually when our Beloved knocks at our heart's door....When we finally run to the door to unlock it, all that is left is the fleeting fragrance of where He *used to be*.

(God's Favorite House, 17-18)

_____

_____

_____

_____

_____

_____

_____

_____

_____

_____

_____

You've not yet seen what happens when I visit a city. Open the door and let Me in!

(*God's Favorite House*, 23)

Day	Date	Time	Location

A Prepared Vessel

We must undergo thorough training and strict discipline, for whatever is untouched in us will be left untouched in others. Moreover we cannot help others to learn lessons which we have not learned before God. The more thorough our training, the greater will be our usefulness in God's work. Correspondingly, the more we spare ourselves—our pride, our narrowness, our happiness—the less our usefulness. If we have covered these things in ourselves, we cannot uncover them in others....The worker is himself first a patient; he must be healed before he can heal others. What he has not seen he cannot show others. Where he has not trodden he cannot lead others. What he has not learned he cannot teach others....

That my feelings may be reliable, I need to pray, "Oh Lord, do not let me go untouched, unbroken and unprepared." I must allow God to work in me what I have never dreamed of, so that I may become a prepared vessel whom He can use.

(Watchman Nee, *The Release of the Spirit*, 41-42)

_____

_____

_____

_____

_____

_____

_____

_____

_____

_____

_____

_____

_____

_____

Watchman Nee was considered a "Seer of the Divine Revelation in the Present Age."

Watchman Nee endured much suffering for the sake of his ministry. He was absolute in following the Lord and faithful in fulfilling his commission. Because he continually fought the battle for the Lord's recovery, he was continually under attack from the enemy.

Watchman Nee was arrested in March 1952. He was judged, falsely condemned, and sentenced to 15 years' imprisonment in 1956. He died in confinement on May 30, 1972.

Along his pathway of following the Lamb, he suffered. Today as a result of his suffering, we have such a rich heritage in the Lord's recovery.

Watchman Nee realized that life is measured not by gain but by loss and that the one who has suffered the most has the most to share with others. For this reason, he never spared himself, but bore the cross and the fellowship of Christ's suffering, being conformed to His death, in order to live Christ out that others might be nourished and enriched with Him. His life is a perfect example that earthly brokenness births heavenly openness. His book, *Spiritual Authority*, is a modern classic.

Day	Date	Time	Location

When the Knocking Stops

The most alarming time is not when God comes to knock on your door. It is *when the knocking stops.* Reality returns with a shock the moment it dawns on us that our Beloved is no longer knocking. We instantly forget the importance of our comforts and lounging lifestyle when the divine knocking stops.

I rose up to open for my beloved, and my hands dripped with myrrh, and my fingers with liquid [sweet-scented] myrrh, [which he had left] upon the handles of the bolt. I opened for my beloved, but my beloved had turned away and withdrawn himself, and was gone! (Song 5:5-6a AMP)...

I'm afraid that if we don't open the door when our Beloved knocks, when the Dove of the Holy Spirit settles; if we fail to open the windows of Heaven through our repentant worship; if we remain unwilling to create an opening for God's glory to enter our world, then at some point *all we will have left is the fragrance of where He used to be.*

(*God's Favorite House*, 18-19)

It's time for **you** *to put your hunger on display.*
(God's Favorite House, 25)

Day	Date	Time	Location

The Spirit of Bartimaeus

Frankly, we all need to be baptized with the spirit of Bartimaeus. This is the blind man who ignored the disapproval of the crowd to cry out to Jesus for mercy (see Mk. 10:46-52). Bartimaeus couldn't see Jesus for himself. He was blind and had to believe in *blind* faith the testimony of someone else who told him, "Jesus is close."...

Sometimes the cares of the day and the weariness of life can temporarily blind us or so numb our senses that we can't perceive the nearness of God. That didn't stop Bartimaeus. Why should it stop us?...

Sometimes all you need to know is that He is near. Hungry cries from your heart will attract Him closer. After all, doesn't God's Word tell us, "The sacrifices of God are a broken spirit: a broken and a contrite heart, O God, Thou wilt not despise"? (Ps. 51:17 KJV) God cannot turn away from brokenness....

Hear me, friend. *You can't preserve your dignity and seek His Deity. You can't save your face and seek His face.* At some point you are going to have to lose your spiritual manners.

(*God's Favorite House*, 21-22)

I'm not going to let You get this close and pass me by. I am desperate for You! Have mercy on me!

(God's Favorite House, 26)

Day	Date	Time	Location

God's Overflowing Love

Our love to God arises out of our emptiness; God's love to us out of His fullness. Our impoverishment draws us to that power which can relieve and to that goodness which can bless us. His overflowing love delights to make us partakers of the bounties He graciously imparts. We can only be said to love God when we endeavour to glorify Him, when we desire a participation of His nature, when we study to imitate His perfections.

We are sometimes inclined to suspect the love of God to us, while we too little suspect our own lack of love to Him....If neglect, forgetfulness, ingratitude, disobedience, coldness in our affections and deadness in our duty are evidences of our lack of love to Him, such evidences we can abundantly show. If life and the catalogue of countless mercies that make life pleasant be proofs of His love to us, these He has given us in abundance. If life eternal, if blessedness that knows no measure and no end, be proofs of love, these He has given us in promise.

(Hannah More, *Religion of the Heart*, 72-73)

Born in 1745 in Bristol, England, **Hannah More** was to become a champion of the disenfranchised of the world. Instead of quiet domesticity, in obscurity, Hannah blazed a trail for women. As a powerful writer she earned a fortune which she used to set up a cottage industry that printed millions of moral tracts that were distributed around the world. She became friends with John Newton, the ex-slave trader, who became her mentor. She joined in with William Wilberforce in the battle against the slave trade.

She has the honor of making English ladies the foremost agent in the education of the poor. The intensity of her love for the Lord Jesus was reflected in a life given for His people.

What an example of balance: the hearts of Mary and Martha beating within the same bosom. Hannah More proves that you can be passionate about His presence and at the same time be a servant to fellow man. She earned credibility in two realms, so that both worlds would heed her invitations. If you build it *He* will come...and *they* will come to see Him.

Day	Date	Time	Location

Hunger or Habit?

One of the keys to turning visitation of the Spirit into habitation of the Spirit is recognizing Him. Has it been so long since you've "seen" Him? Would you recognize Him if He comes on a colt instead of a stallion? Would you embrace His visitation in humility as much as in power?...

Why don't you forget about your manners right now? It is time to lay aside your religious protocols, the things that dictate what is supposed to happen and when. *God has always preferred spiritual hunger over spiritual ritual.* Are you going to miss your moment? If you can feel Him edging closer and closer, then don't let Him get this close and pass you by...Remember that *God is shopping for a place to break out.* He is knocking at the door. I can almost hear Him say to us, "*You know what happens when I visit a church.* **You've not yet seen what happens when I visit a city. Open the door and let Me in!**"

(God's Favorite House, 23-24)

We welcome God's visitation, but our real desire is for habitation.

(*God's Favorite House*, 48)

Day	Date	Time	Location

The Covering of Repentance

Complete moral purity can only describe God. Everything that appears to be good among men and women must be discounted, for we are human. Not one of us is morally pure. Abraham, David and Elijah; Moses, Peter and Paul—all were good men. They were included in God's fellowship. But each had his human flaws and weaknesses as members of Adam's race. Each had to find the place of humble repentance. Because God knows our hearts and our intentions, He is able to restore His sincere and believing children who are in the faith.

Much of our problem in continuing fellowship with a holy God is that many Christians repent only for what they do, rather than for what they are.

(A. W. Tozer, Whatever Happened to Worship?, 72.)

When God *really* shows up, I don't care what your title is or how long you've known Him, you suddenly become aware of the need to cover yourself in repentance. It is because of the weightiness of His approaching glory....

Every time this has happened in my experience and in Church history, "God came down" as a result of repentance and desperation in the atmosphere of worship. I can promise you that church programs will never accomplish this. *True revival comes when the Reviver comes to town!*

(God's Favorite House, 30)

_____

_____

_____

_____

_____

_____

_____

*Have you learned to look at sin and everything that comes short of the glory of God, as a **wound to the heart of Jesus**?*

(Jessie Penn-Lewis, *Opened Heavens*, 25)

GOD'S *Favorite* HOUSE JOURNAL

Day	Date	Time	Location

Godly Awe, Godly Fear

What does this mean to us spiritually? The light of God searching our worship. Is there sin in our worship? Is there sacrilege in our holy things? Oh, the flippant talking about sacred things, instead of hush and reverence and godly awe. There is a flippant using of the Name of the Lord as we would use other people's names. Does it mean that we are not to speak His Name? Nay, but there should come upon us a reverent hush in speaking it, because we never lose the presence of the Holy One....If there is anything that is lacking today, it is godly awe, and godly fear.

(Jessie Penn-Lewis, *Opened Heavens*, 26-27)

In the realm of prayer and revival, a way to open the windows of Heaven is to break vessels and release torrents of repentance and worship among the people of God on earth. There has to be a deep brokenness in us if we want to break through and see an open window in Heaven. *Brokenness on earth creates openness in Heaven!*

(*God's Favorite House*, 31)

Tears turn on the faucet of God's compassion.
(God's Favorite House, 21)

Day	Date	Time	Location

The Fragrance of Brokenness

     The Bible tells of the pure spikenard [see Mk. 14:3]. God purposely used this term "pure" in His Word to show that it is truly spiritual. But if the alabaster box is not broken, the pure spikenard will not flow forth. Strange to say, many are still treasuring the alabaster box, thinking that its value exceeds that of the ointment. Many think that their outward man [the body] is more precious than their inward man [the spirit]. This becomes the problem in the Church….However, we are not antique collectors; we are not vase admirers; we are those who desire to smell only the fragrance of the ointment. Without the breaking of the outward, the inward will not come forth. Thus individually we have no flowing out, but even the Church does not have a living way. Why then should we hold ourselves so precious, if our outward contains instead of releases the fragrance?…So the Treasure is in the earthen vessel, but if the earthen vessel is not broken, who can see the Treasure within?

(Watchman Nee, The Release of the Spirit, 12-13)

     "The sacrifices of God are a broken spirit: a broken and a contrite heart, O God, Thou wilt not despise." This is **the costly key that unlocks the riches of God's presence!** This is the fragrance God cannot ignore. He will respond. The brass heavens will be broken!

(God's Favorite House, 32-33)

It is a great thing to let God so break us that He can break others through us.

(Jessie Penn-Lewis, *Opened Heavens*, 45)

Day	Date	Time	Location

The Ultimate Issue

Firstly, then, the ultimate issue in this universe. It is summed up in one word, a very comprehensive word including many things, an all-embracing word. It is the word "worship." That is the ultimate issue in this universe to which all else is related, and which governs all that has been revealed in the Word of God as God's way of reaching His end. As we approach this matter of worship, standing back from the detail and from all the form, the means used temporarily to set it forth, we recognize that it is set in a realm far bigger than this earth. It embraces other realms, its setting is super-earthly....

There is nothing here of two realms that you might call secular and spiritual, no two realms in this universe, it is spiritual altogether....

It is the question which arises with us continually, all the way through our lives, in every connection. What place has God in this, where does God come in? How does satan stand to get an advantage here?...Who is going to be worshiped alone, without reserve, without dividedness, without question, without rival and without grudging?—whole-hearted, unquestioning worship!

(T. Austin Sparks, *The Ultimate Issue of the Universe*, 6-7, 11, 12)

In 1905 at the age of 17 on a cold, darkened street corner in Glasgow, Scotland, **T. Austin Sparks** gave his heart to the Lord. It was a commitment from which he would never withdraw. He also took every advantage to go and hear the great preachers of his day, including Dr. G. Campbell Morgan and F.B. Meyer, who was to become a firm friend and counselor.

In 1921 he took charge of the Honor Oak Baptist church. It was from Honor Oak that he became more widely known as a gifted Bible teacher. There was a strong emphasis on the believers' life in the Spirit, the eternal purpose of God in His Son, and the heavenly nature of the Church.

Such was the special calling of T. Austin Sparks, a man plowing a furrow perhaps a little apart from his contemporaries but always true to Christ Jesus his Savior and Lord.

As a pioneer of pursuing a deeper life in God, he raised the bar higher than many followers of Christ. He wasn't happy just to follow—he was insistent to follow more closely. The power of proximity opened divine revelation to T.A. Sparks just as it had to John the beloved who leaned on the breast of Jesus.

Day	Date	Time	Location

Holy Sweat

Christians around the world are saying, "We want revival; we want a move of God." Unfortunately, we haven't learned from David's mistakes. Often we try to do the same thing he did the first time he attempted to bring God's presence to Jerusalem [see 2 Sam. 6:2-10]. We cram the holy things of God on a new cart of man's making, thinking God will be pleased. Then we are shocked when we discover His disdain! He won't let oxen pull on carts carrying His glory! We expect somebody or something else to "sweat" out the hard part of revival. All we want to do is sing and dance in the procession. These half-baked, man-centered revival celebrations go as smoothly as David's first "ark party"—until we hit a God-bump at Nachon's threshing floor....

Uzzah died after he tried to stabilize what God had shaken. We still insist on smoothing out the bumps and rounding off the edges of God's commandment. We are futilely trying to create an "Uzzah-friendly" environment when we prize man's comfort above God's comfort. I often put it this way: *"Seeker-friendly is fine, but Spirit-friendly is fire!"*...David learned the hard way that God doesn't think like men do. His ways—*and the road to a holy revival*—are higher and "sweatier."

(*God's Favorite House*, 33-34)

_____

_____

_____

_____

_____

_____

_____

_____

_____

No more oxen.... The weakness of man is what will carry the ark of God's presence.

(*God's Favorite House*, 34)

Day	Date	Time	Location

Participation—The Price of His Presence

When David made his second attempt to bring the ark to Jerusalem, he carefully followed God's instructions. God didn't want a cart of wood or an ox carrying His presence—He wanted real men....The Levites had to carry the heavy ark on their shoulders for a journey of an estimated ten miles. Those men must have sweated!...The Levites would kill an ox and a fattened calf, move forward six paces, and go through the sacrificial process again....David and his procession...put in some heavy labor on the road to revival....They didn't walk through the gates of Jerusalem looking fresh and sharp in their "church" clothes shouting, "Hey, look at us. We're having revival!"

David and his procession of Levites, priests, and worshipers paid a dear price to usher God's presence into their city that day....Most people go for the new cart method because it represents a low-cost, no-sweat method of worship....

I'm concerned that most Christians aren't interested in paying any price for God's presence. We expect it to be brought to us on a silver platter. We are like spectators watching paid performers, or oxen, trying to drag God's presence into church. *It is time to abandon spectator-based services. Become a participator!*

(*God's Favorite House*, 34-36)

_____

_____

_____

_____

_____

_____

_____

_____

True revival comes when the Reviver comes to town!

(*God's Favorite House*, 30)

Day	Date	Time	Location

Made for Worship

God, being the God He was and is, and being infinitely perfect and infinitely beautiful and infinitely glorious and infinitely admirable and infinitely loving, out of His own inward necessity had to have some creature that was capable of admiring Him and loving Him and knowing Him. So God made man in His own image; in the image and likeness of God made He him; and He made him as near to being like Himself as it was possible for the creature to be like the Creator. The most godlike thing in the universe is the soul of man.

The reason God made man in His image was that He might appreciate God and admire and adore and worship; so that God might not be a picture, so to speak, hanging in a gallery with nobody looking at Him. He might not be a flower that no one could smell; He might not be a star that no one can see. God made somebody to smell that flower, the lily of the valley. He wanted someone to see that glorious image. He wanted someone to see the star, so He made us and in making us He made us to worship Him.

(A.W. Tozer, *Worship: The Missing Jewel of the Evangelical Church*, 7-8)

Fellowship *is more than partnership; it is a blending of spirit with spirit, of heart with heart, so that no words are needed, for the two are one.*
(Jessie Penn-Lewis, *Face to Face*, 46)

Day	Date	Time	Location

Blessed Are Those Who Hunger

The way to open the heavens above you is for you to pursue a fresh revelation of where God is. We live with less than God's best most of the time because we tend to major on the truth of where God has been. This revelation must be pursued because God doesn't feed casual nibblers. He feeds the hungry. When He does reveal Himself to you or to me, that revelation will never take away from past truths; it will only add to them....

I believe that God is constantly giving us new revelations of His Person. This is partly because our unchanging God is continually moving and working among His ever-changing people....

Always remember that *the truths of God are meant to lead us to the God of truth,* the Person of who He is. God wants you to follow these tracks of truth until you come to a revelation of who He is. ***Thirty seconds of beholding the glory of Jesus through an opening in the heavenlies transformed a murderous Saul into the martyr named Paul. That's the power of an open Heaven!***

(*God's Favorite House*, 38-40)

_____

_____

_____

_____

_____

_____

_____

_____

_____

_____

_____

God isn't obligated to feed casual nibblers.
(God's Favorite House, 38)

| Day | Date | Time | Location |

The Incense of Worship

Throughout the Bible, when the heavens opened and the glory of God appeared, a cloud was often involved. When God chooses to visit humanity, He brings His cloud for our protection. The cloud shields us from seeing too much lest we see His face and die. We are close but covered. *When **you** choose to **visit God**, you have to make your own cloud....*

It is the blood of Jesus Christ that gives us *access* to God's throne room today, but it is our sacrificial, repentant worship that *attracts* Him and allows Him to move *close* to us. In the same way, true worship makes enough smoke to allow you to draw close to Him. Worship is the key component to the manifest presence of God coming down among us.

When you worship, you are "making smoke" as a sweet incense, a favorite fragrance, to attract His presence. If you make enough smoke, His mercy will cover you and God can come even nearer to you, and you can draw near to Him. The "worship cloud" releases His covering mercy so you can commune with Him in an intimacy and nearness that can't be created at any other time.

(God's Favorite House, 40-41)

_____

_____

_____

_____

_____

_____

_____

_____

_____

_____

Prayer sprinkled on passion makes smoke.
(*God's Favorite House*, 41)

Day	Date	Time	Location

The Weightiness of Glory

In the Old Testament, the Hebrew word translated as "glory" is *kabod*. It literally means weightiness or weighty splendor....*I wonder how many times the "weighty glory" of God has visited us but not come in?*...Why won't He stay?...

The answer is very simple: *We haven't built a mercy seat to hold the glory of God.* There is no place for Him to sit! What is comfortable to you and I is not comfortable to the *kabod*, the weightiness of God. We are happy to sit in our comfortable spiritual recliners all day, but the seat of God, the mercy seat, is a little different. It is the only seat on earth that can bear the weight of His glory and compel Him to come in and *stay*.

God is looking for a church that has learned how to build a mercy seat for His glory. When He finds a house that has paid the price to build Him a resting place, He will come and He will stay. That is when we will see a revival that is unlike any we have ever seen before.

(*God's Favorite House*, 49)

Build a mercy seat!

(God's Favorite House, 61)

Day	Date	Time	Location

An Overflow of Praise

Today we praise God for the fact that our glorious Jesus is the risen Christ. A church that doesn't know how to pray and shout will never be shaken. It is only when people have learned the secret of prayer, of power and of praise, that God comes forth.

Some people say, "Well, I praise God inwardly." But if there is an abundance of praise in our hearts, our mouths cannot help speaking it.

The praise cannot come out unless it is inside. There must first be the inner working of the power of God; it is He who changes the heart and transforms the life. Before there is any outward evidence there must be the inflow of divine life. When people come and pray and praise as the early disciples did, there will be something doing. People who come will catch fire and want to come again. They will have no use for a place where everything has been formal, dry, and dead.

(Smith Wigglesworth, quoted in *Promises for Spirit-Led Living*, 141, 145)

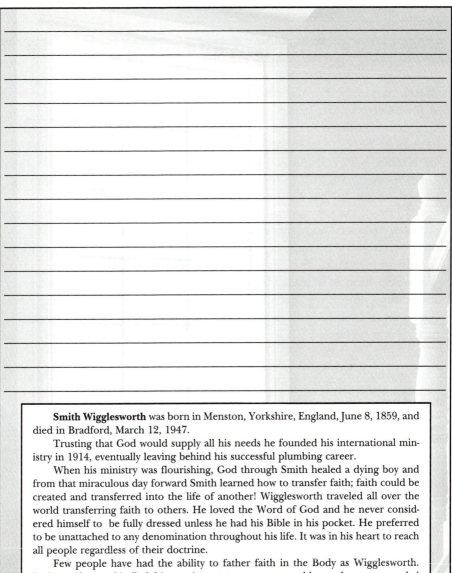

Smith Wigglesworth was born in Menston, Yorkshire, England, June 8, 1859, and died in Bradford, March 12, 1947.

Trusting that God would supply all his needs he founded his international ministry in 1914, eventually leaving behind his successful plumbing career.

When his ministry was flourishing, God through Smith healed a dying boy and from that miraculous day forward Smith learned how to transfer faith; faith could be created and transferred into the life of another! Wigglesworth traveled all over the world transferring faith to others. He loved the Word of God and he never considered himself to be fully dressed unless he had his Bible in his pocket. He preferred to be unattached to any denomination throughout his life. It was in his heart to reach all people regardless of their doctrine.

Few people have had the ability to father faith in the Body as Wigglesworth. Perhaps if we rekindled his passionate prayers, we could see the same results! Wigglesworth was passionate to a fault! May my faults and deficiencies be in the same area.

GOD'S *Favorite* HOUSE JOURNAL

Day	Date	Time	Location

The Components of True Worship

We all need to learn from King David's experiences as a God chaser. We know he met disaster in his first attempt to return the ark to Jerusalem, but he was successful his second time around....

David did two things to make sure God's presence remained in Jerusalem. First, he prepared a place for God's presence by constructing a tabernacle without walls or a veil. Second, he...created a "living" mercy seat of worship in the tabernacle so God would be pleased to sit and remain in that humble sanctuary....

The way we can build a mercy seat is to take our positions as purified, "beaten" worshipers. One problem is that God still requires mercy seat worshipers to be formed of gold tried in the fire (purified), conformed (beaten) into the image of perfection, and moved into the proper position of unity for worship. This speaks of purity, brokenness, and unity—the three components of true worship under the new covenant of the blood of Jesus. *Brokenness on the earth creates openness in the heavens.*

(*God's Favorite House*, 51-52)

Once the outward man is broken, man's spirit very naturally abides in the presence of God without ceasing.

(Watchman Nee, *The Release of the Spirit*, 23)

Day	Date	Time	Location

The Wings of Worship

Too many of us just want to be pre-formed or pre-cast in a quick and easy "one-two-three revival formula." I can't give that to you. However, I can tell you that your wings of worship can be created only one way. They must be beaten into the proper position and the proper image. *The hammer blows of life will bend us "Godward" if our responses to life's challenges are right.* Sometimes we respond wrongly to what life sends us; then the adversity beats us out of position. *Instead of becoming "better" we become "bitter."* This means that our wings of worship will not be where they are supposed to be; they will be in the right place but in the wrong position—in church but with a wrong attitude.

God intends for the hammer blows of life to move your wings of worship into position so as to create one who "in all things gives thanks" [see 1 Thess. 5:18]....

When the worshipers around the mercy seat come into *their* position, God can move into *His* position and occupy the middle ground between them.

(God's Favorite House, 53)

Thanksgiving gets you in the gates, praise gets you in the courts, but worship takes you into His presence.

(God's Favorite House, 42)

Day	Date	Time	Location

Where Are the Worshipers?

Even though the cherubim on the ark amounted to a "cheap earthly imitation" of the heavenly reality, there is still so much mystique about the ark that Hollywood producers made millions of dollars simply by talking about the "lost ark" in an adventure film.

When will the Church realize that God isn't looking for the lost ark; He knows where that is. *He is looking for "the lost worshipers"* so He can replace the lost glory in the earth. (*God's Favorite House*, 54)

The purpose of God in sending His Son to die and rise and live and be at the right hand of God the Father was that He might restore to us the missing jewel, the jewel of worship; that we might come back and learn to do again that which we were created to do in the first place—worship the Lord in the beauty of holiness, to spend our time in awesome wonder and adoration of God, feeling and expressing it, and letting it get into our labors and doing nothing except as an act of worship to Almighty God through His Son Jesus Christ.

(A. W. Tozer, *Worship: The Missing Jewel of the Evangelical Church*, 12)

God wants worshipers first. Jesus did not redeem us to make us workers; He redeemed us to make us worshipers.

(A. W. Tozer, *Tozer on Worship and Entertainment*, 19)

Day	Date	Time	Location

In the Image of Christ

Those who follow Christ are destined to bear his image, and to be the brethren of the firstborn Son of God. Their goal is to become "as Christ." Christ's followers always have his image before their eyes, and in its light all other images are screened from their sight. It penetrates into the depths of their being, fills them, and makes them more and more like their Master. The image of Jesus Christ impresses itself in daily communion on the image of the disciple. No follower of Jesus can contemplate his image in a spirit of cold detachment. That image has the power to transform our lives, and if we surrender ourselves utterly to him, we cannot help bearing his image ourselves. We become the sons of God, we stand side by side with Christ, our unseen Brother, bearing like him the image of God....

Here, right from the beginning, is the mysterious paradox of man. He is a creature, and yet he is destined to be like his Creator. Created man is destined to bear the image of uncreated God.

(Dietrich Bonhoeffer, *The Cost of Discipleship*, 337-338)

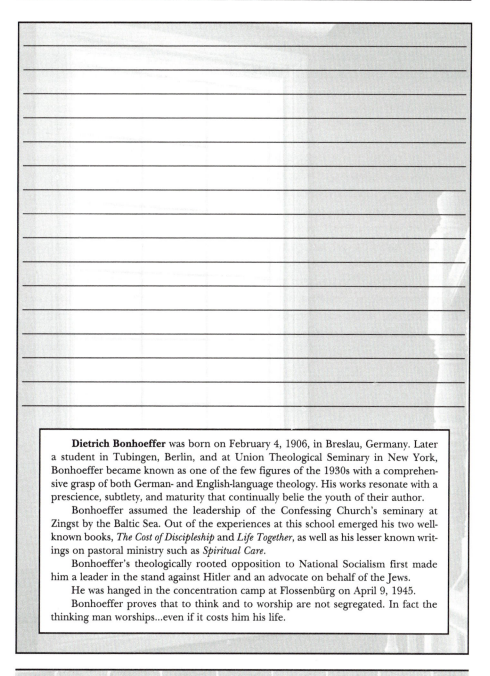

Dietrich Bonhoeffer was born on February 4, 1906, in Breslau, Germany. Later a student in Tubingen, Berlin, and at Union Theological Seminary in New York, Bonhoeffer became known as one of the few figures of the 1930s with a comprehensive grasp of both German- and English-language theology. His works resonate with a prescience, subtlety, and maturity that continually belie the youth of their author.

Bonhoeffer assumed the leadership of the Confessing Church's seminary at Zingst by the Baltic Sea. Out of the experiences at this school emerged his two well-known books, *The Cost of Discipleship* and *Life Together*, as well as his lesser known writings on pastoral ministry such as *Spiritual Care*.

Bonhoeffer's theologically rooted opposition to National Socialism first made him a leader in the stand against Hitler and an advocate on behalf of the Jews.

He was hanged in the concentration camp at Flossenbürg on April 9, 1945.

Bonhoeffer proves that to think and to worship are not segregated. In fact the thinking man worships...even if it costs him his life.

Day	Date	Time	Location

Preparing to Greet the King

When we worship in spirit and in truth, the glory of God will come. What we will experience at that point is simply a precursor of what will happen on that great day when the King of Glory personally returns to the earth for the second time. The first time He came, He carried His glory lightly because He walked in humility. He tiptoed through our world so He would not disturb His creation, much as an adult tiptoes through a child's playroom to avoid breaking the toys.

The next time Jesus appears, He will be astride a horse and will come in unrestrained power and authority to repossess the entire house. When His feet touch the top of the Mount of Olives, His *kabod*, His weighty glory, will be so great that the Mount of Olives will literally split in two. The eastern gate will suddenly open to allow His "real" triumphant entry. *The first was just the rehearsal.* **Next time He will be in costume!** And every knee will bow and every tongue will confess that Jesus Christ is Lord [see Phil. 2:10-11].

(God's Favorite House, 55)

_____

_____

_____

_____

_____

_____

_____

_____

_____

_____

_____

_____

Only one opinion matters.

(*God's Favorite House*, 58)

Day	Date	Time	Location

Hosting the Holy Ghost

How can we recreate or "compete" with the kind of worship God receives in Heaven?...Remember that you can beg for God to come all you want, but until you prepare a place where His weighty glory can safely dwell, He may visit but He cannot stay. I don't know about you, but I am tired of visits. Somehow we have to reclaim the ability to *host the Holy Ghost*. David knew how to do it.

David instructed sanctified Levites to keep fueling the flame of God's presence with 24-hour worship every day....

David surrounded that ark with worshipers so that the glory of God would keep flickering. For the first time in history, Israelites, pagans, or heathen could stand near Mount Zion in Jerusalem and literally see the blue flame of God's glory flickering between the outstretched arms and dancing feet of the worshipers in David's tabernacle! How could this be? It was because David's tabernacle was a place marked by open-veiled and unfettered worship....

David did more than surround the ark of God with sanctified worshipers. He made sure that their primary focus was to minister to God through praise, worship, and adoration.

(God's Favorite House, 56-58)

It is time to abandon spectator-based services.
Become a participator!

Day	Date	Time	Location

Step Into the Weeping Zone

Some people say that you can become so heavenly minded that you are no earthly good, but I'm not sure that is possible. In fact, that phrase is a good description of the "weeping zone," that place between the porch of man and the altar of God. Can I tell you what you do in that position? *The weeping zone is the place of intercession before God's throne* where you step into the gap to intercede for others.

God has a heart to see all men saved, but He depends on you and me to fulfill our ministry of reconciliation in the weeping zone. He has called us to become bridges between the kingdom of light and the kingdom of darkness. The greatest Bridge of all is Jesus Christ, our great High Priest who ever lives to intercede for us before the Father [see Heb. 7:25]. When you and I enter the weeping zone, we come alongside the Great Intercessor and face the throne, reaching out for God with one hand and for man with the other. We are called to intercede in worship until God and man have met together.

(*God's Favorite House*, 59)

Brokenness on earth creates openness in Heaven!
(God's Favorite House, 30)

Day	Date	Time	Location

A Place Fitting for God to Dwell

You must begin by seeing that each of our souls is like a splendid castle. The castle is fashioned entirely out of the clearest crystal—better still, out of diamond. Because of this, you and everyone around you may look within the very center, to the throne room itself, to the seat of majesty where one sovereign authority reigns over all that you do.........While He is within us, He is still, also, the high and holy Creator and we are His creations. And there is a vast difference between our comprehension and His. He is Spirit, and we are flesh. How can we ever create with our own hands, by our poor efforts, a place fitting for His Majesty, since we cannot form the slightest conception on our own?......In short, we start by allowing our sovereign King to govern—and in this way we begin to see, as through a mist, the first dim outlines of the castle He longs to reveal within us—an interior dwelling place of sublime dignity and great beauty.

(Teresa of Ávila, from *The Interior Castle*, quoted in *Majestic Is Your Name*, 24-26)

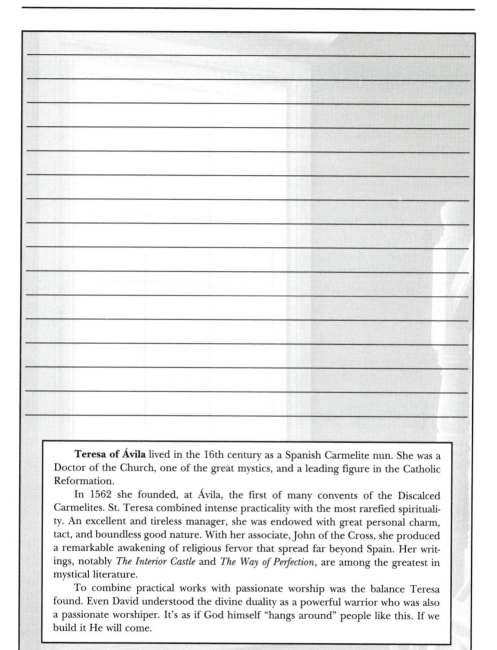

Teresa of Ávila lived in the 16th century as a Spanish Carmelite nun. She was a Doctor of the Church, one of the great mystics, and a leading figure in the Catholic Reformation.

In 1562 she founded, at Ávila, the first of many convents of the Discalced Carmelites. St. Teresa combined intense practicality with the most rarefied spirituality. An excellent and tireless manager, she was endowed with great personal charm, tact, and boundless good nature. With her associate, John of the Cross, she produced a remarkable awakening of religious fervor that spread far beyond Spain. Her writings, notably *The Interior Castle* and *The Way of Perfection*, are among the greatest in mystical literature.

To combine practical works with passionate worship was the balance Teresa found. Even David understood the divine duality as a powerful warrior who was also a passionate worshiper. It's as if God himself "hangs around" people like this. If we build it He will come.

Day	Date	Time	Location

People of the Gap

The world needs God's grace, but His truth is attached to it....His truth is equivalent to His *judgment,* and apart from God's grace through Jesus Christ, none of us have a chance. That means that if God's manifest presence—the thing we are praying for—rushes out and encounters unrepentant flesh, then the truth or judgment of God will instantly obliterate it just as light obliterates darkness....

When God's people become worshipers and stand in the gap, *they "filter" the truth and judgment component of glory.* That means that the only component of God's glory that rushes past them to flow in the streets of the city is grace and mercy....

Our cities don't need better sermons or better songs. They need "gap people" who can reach for God with one hand and for the world with the other. Are you called to take a stand in the weeping zone? Can you forget what man says while reaching out to God with one hand in repentant, broken worship and reaching out to unredeemed man with the other?...

Do you really want revival? *Build a mercy seat for God.*

(*God's Favorite House,* 60-61)

_____

_____

_____

_____

_____

_____

_____

_____

_____

_____

_____

_____

It is in the "secret place of the Most High" that we learn to "pour out"...

(Jessie Penn-Lewis, *Communion with God*, 53)

Day	Date	Time	Location

The Light of His Glory

If we can just turn on the light of His glory, then suddenly everyone will see and know the difference between truth and error. Most people will choose truth when given the opportunity; it is just that *they have never had enough light around them to see the way.* The light of God's glory existed before the sun and moon, and it will continue to exist after they have been snuffed out. Somehow it must be made manifest!

Once we find out how to turn on the light of God's glory, we can determine how to *keep* that spiritual light shining. *This is what I call an open heaven!* We must keep the heavens open over that place of easy access to God's presence....For generations, we have struggled to free the lost from satan's bondage using the anointing. God has opened the door for us to do it much quicker and easier through the revelation of *His glory* in our lives and churches.

(God's Favorite House, 64)

When we worship in spirit and in truth, the glory of God will come.

(*God's Favorite House*, 55)

Day	Date	Time	Location

Holiness Is the Mark

Holiness is a state of soul in which all the powers of the body and mind are consciously given up to God; and the witness of holiness is that testimony which the Holy Spirit bears with our spirit that the offering is accepted through Christ. The work is accomplished the moment we lay our all upon the altar. Under the old covenant dispensation it was ordained by God that whatsoever touched the altar should be holy....

Will you come, dear disciple of Jesus, and venture even *now* to lay your all upon this blessed altar?...

Remember, "The just shall live by *faith*," not *ecstasies*. *HOLINESS is the mark; that state of soul in which all the powers of soul and body are consciously given up to God.*...Neither former unfaithfulness nor present unworthiness need hinder your coming *just as you are*. The blood of Jesus cleanseth from all sin.

(Phoebe Palmer, *Entire Devotion to God*, 21-22)

Phoebe Palmer was born in 1807 and died in 1874. She is considered to be "The Mother of the Holiness Movement." This movement began in 1835 with her Tuesday Meetings for the Promotion of Holiness, which continued for 39 years in New York City, where she lived with her physician husband. The success of Phoebe Palmer's informal meetings encouraged other women to conduct the same type of ministry, and dozens of them sprang up throughout North America.

In the fall of 1857, she and her husband traveled to Hamilton, Ontario. There they attracted crowds of several thousand people when an afternoon prayer meeting became a ten-day revival meeting during which four hundred people were converted to Christ. They experienced similar successes in New York City and in England, where they preached for four years to packed houses. It is estimated that within her lifetime, Phoebe Palmer brought over 25,000 people to faith in Christ.

Often our focus has been to affect people and by that impress God. By pursuing Christ, Phoebe affected people. Our primary ministry is to Him. To be holy and acceptable to Him is the ultimate call.

Day	Date	Time	Location

The Light of His Presence

When someone pays the price to open the windows of Heaven through sacrificial, repentant worship, the light of God's manifested presence beams across the dreary landscape of human souls and lets everybody know that it's time to be free. This is what the prophet Isaiah meant when he prophesied of Christ's coming: "The people who walked in darkness have seen a great light; those who dwelt in the land of the shadow of death, upon them a light has shined [Is. 9:2 NKJV].

You know that you have encountered the pure presence of God as a result of an open heaven when people who live in "the land of the shadow of death" see a great light. *This is the manifested presence of God.* When the heavens open over a city or nation, there is a heightened sense of the presence of God on the earth. This is the ultimate form of "spiritual warfare."...

When His manifested presence appears in any area or vicinity, the forces of darkness lose their ability to sway the public.

(God's Favorite House, 65-66)

There is no better way to wage spiritual warfare than to turn on the light of God's glory by ushering in His manifest presence.

(God's Favorite House, 72)

Day	Date	Time	Location

Let's Evict the Devil!

There is a place for Bible-based, Spirit-led binding and loosing by the saints, but most of the time we concentrate on the binding....

We should *loose something in the heavenly realm* every time we feel led to bind something on earth. Never pray to bind the devil unless you also pray to loose the power of Jesus and the Spirit of God in that situation. *If you bind one thing and don't loose something else, you really haven't done anything but tie everything up in knots.* **Whenever I pray that God would "open the windows of Heaven," I also pray that He would close "the gates of hell!"**

When Jesus said, "the gates of hell shall not prevail," He meant that they don't have authority over the redeemed or God's Kingdom [see Mt. 16:18]. When the gates of Heaven open, it is time to storm the enemy's gates and *plunder hell to populate Heaven*. It helps us to know that satan no longer has possession of the "keys to hell." Jesus recovered them! *Satan can't even lock the doors to his own house!*

(*God's Favorite House*, 68-69)

Satan is occupying; he doesn't own.
(*God's Favorite House*, 70)

Day	Date	Time	Location

Bargain Basement Blessings

God's people need more than just another "good meeting" that sends goose bumps up and down their spines. *We need a God-meeting that leaves us with a limp!* Where are the Jacobs who will lay hold on the theophany of God and wrestle with their destiny until it is changed? Who will take hold of God and say, "I am not going to let go until You bless me"?...

All too often we approach God with a discount store mentality. Whether we come for revival, physical healing, or a financial blessing, we hope to get what we want at the cheapest price in the shortest time possible. I don't know about you, but I have never seen God do things that way. We like to line up like we've found some celestial "blue-light special" with our lists of prayers and petitions. Then we say, "Bless me." I have begun to pray that God would not answer our exact requests, but answer according to our need instead. We know what we want—*but do we know what we need?*

(*God's Favorite House*, 75-76)

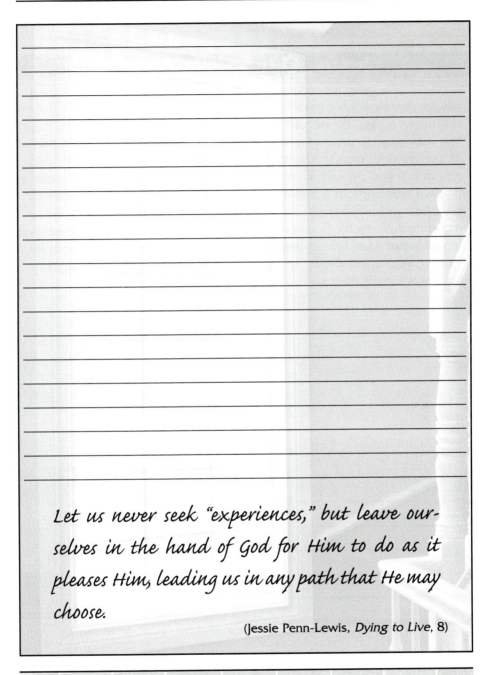

Let us never seek "experiences," but leave ourselves in the hand of God for Him to do as it
pleases Him, leading us in any path that He may
choose.

(Jessie Penn-Lewis, *Dying to Live*, 8)

Day	Date	Time	Location

Jesus, Our Special Love

It is a great art to know how to converse with Jesus, and great wisdom to know how to keep Him. Be humble and peaceful, and Jesus will be with you. Be devout and calm, and He will remain with you. You may quickly drive Him away and lose His grace, if you turn back to the outside world. And if you drive Him away and lose Him, to whom will you go and whom will you then seek as a friend? You cannot live well without a friend, and if Jesus be not your friend above all else, you will be very sad and desolate. Thus, you are acting foolishly if you trust or rejoice in any other. Choose the opposition of the whole world rather than offend Jesus. Of all those who are dear to you, let Him be your special love. Let all things be loved for the sake of Jesus, but Jesus for His own sake.

(Thomas à Kempis, *The Imitation of Christ*, http://www.ccel.org/k/kempis/imitation/imitation.htm)

_____

_____

_____

_____

_____

_____

_____

_____

_____

_____

_____

_____

_____

_____

_____

_____

_____

_____

_____

_____

_____

Thomas à Kempis was born in 1379 and died in 1471. In the Netherlands, he became an Augustinian priest. The great devotional work of his life was *The Imitation of Christ*.

Thomas found a "new devotion" in Deventer, which was the focus and center of a revival in the Low Countries of Germany in the fourteenth century of the same fervor as the primitive Christians at Jerusalem and Antioch in the first century. He was part of a community called the "Brothers and Sisters of the Common Life." They took no vows, but lived a life of poverty, chastity, and obedience. He was a part of this group until his untimely death, at the early age of 43. Thomas à Kempis' favorite subjects were the mystery of our Redemption, and the love of Jesus Christ as shown in His words and works.

If the "fulness....indwells Christ," as he wrote, then we can create the same indwelling by the "Imitation of Christ."

Day	Date	Time	Location

Mortally Wounded

The Church has been strutting down the sidewalks of the world in arrogance, pointing fingers of incrimination in every direction and telling everybody else to "get right." Meanwhile, we have a proverbial board sticking out of our own eye that is a mile long. It is time for us to say, "God, I don't know whether You will bring a *blessing* or a *changing*, but something has to happen. Teach us how to build mercy seats instead of judgment seats."

We need to have encounters with God that leave us changed forever. *I am tired of coming to church and getting touched but not changed.* We must lock onto the presence of God and say, "I'm not letting You go until something happens inside me and I am never the same again."

This is the God-kind-of-change that permanently wounds the old man and the old ways of doing things. It causes the death of something within us, which marks a change for the better. People should see us coming with a new limp, a new *tenderness born of the day we lost our wrestling contest with God.*

(*God's Favorite House*, 78)

_____

_____

_____

_____

_____

_____

_____

_____

_____

_____

_____

Never trust anybody who doesn't walk with a limp.

(*God's Favorite House*, 78)

Day	Date	Time	Location

Presence Over Presents

How often we come to church services to present our petitions, prophesy this, and say that, while God says, "Is there anybody here who just wants Me?"

The highest level of worship is when we push aside His hands and pursue His face! *His face means His favor.*...For how long has the Church not been pursuing the true favor of God?...

We must mature to the point that we can say, "It's not His hands," and push His hands aside to seek His face and say, "I'll be a servant" and "I just want to be where you are." Then our worship is no longer self-serving to get something; instead we begin to just give everything to Him. Instead of "bless me," it becomes "bless Him"! We no longer give to get, but we give out of passion!...

God is also determined to change the way we "have church." *Presence over presents!* He longs for the worshiper who will go after the "Giver" more than the "gifts"! Are you that person? Are you a restorer of God's favorite house?

(God's Favorite House, 82-83)

We are called to an everlasting preoccupation with God.

(A. W. Tozer, from *That Incredible Christian*, quoted in *Gems From Tozer*, 13)

Day	Date	Time	Location

Less Than the Best

I sometimes wonder what happened to the true worship *leaders* whose sole purpose is to lead God's people into His presence for *His* sake?

The anointing can easily draw a big crowd, but the problem with those types of man meetings is that you can curry the favor of men without ever seeking the favor of God....

I am afraid that most of our carefully orchestrated church services and revival meetings would go along just fine without God's help, approval, or appearance....It's a statement on our low hunger level that we would be satisfied with less of God than He wants us to experience.

We have practiced and perfected the art of entertaining man, but along the way we have lost the art of entertaining God.... Sometimes we get so involved in attracting man to our outstretched hand that we lose the desire and the ability to attract God with the other. When you can pull men toward you but you can't get God to come close anymore, the temptation is to keep promising Him though you can't deliver Him.

(God's Favorite House, 87-88)

Seek the face of God. Lose the fear of man—and gain the fear of God.

(God's Favorite House, 57)

Day	Date	Time	Location

The Soul's Real Desire

Again, we have some higher, nobler desires of the Spirit which cannot be fulfilled in this world. Therefore there must be another spiritual world in which those desires can be met. This material world cannot by any means satisfy our spiritual cravings.

The soul's real desire can only be satisfied by God who has created the soul and the desire for him inherent in it. Because God has created man in his own likeness, man has in him something of the divine nature which longs for fellowship with him. Like seeks like by the laws of being. And when we are rooted in the Eternal Being, we shall not only feel satisfied, but also have eternal life in him.

(Sadhu Sundar Singh, from *Reality and Religion*, quoted in *Sadhu Sundar Singh: A Biography*, 10)

*We perpetually over-promise and under-produce....*Only God Himself can satisfy the hunger He placed within us. *His hand can supply our needs, but only His face can satisfy our deepest longings.* As we look upon His face, we are brought into union with our destiny, and we enjoy the favor of His loving gaze and the incomparable kiss of His lips.

(*God's Favorite House*, 89)

Sundar Singh was born in 1889 into an important landowning Sikh family in North India. Sundar Singh's mother took great care in his religious development at the feet of an ascetic holy man.

Her death when he was 14 plunged him into violence and despair. In final defiance of the missionaries' religion, he bought a Bible and burned it page by page in his home compound while his friends watched. That same night he went to his room determined to commit suicide on a railway line.

However, during the night, like the apostle Paul he had a vision of the Lord Jesus Who asked Sundar why he was persecuting Him. Henceforth he would follow Christ forever.

For the next 25 years he would witness heroically for his Lord. All his talks and personal speech sprang out of his profound early morning meditation, especially on the Gospels. To the end of his life he remained a man who sought nothing for himself, but only the opportunity to offer Christ to everyone.

If you can ever see Him you'll follow Him. Ask Sadhu or Paul! Passionate worship may help you get a greater glimpse of His glory. Build the place of passionate praise!

GOD'S *Favorite* HOUSE JOURNAL

Day	Date	Time	Location

No Fear, No Worship

Worship means "to feel in the heart"...A person that merely goes through the form and doesn't feel anything is not worshiping.

Worship also means to "express in some appropriate manner" what you feel....

And what will be expressed? "A humbling but delightful sense of admiring awe and astonished wonder." It is delightful to worship God, but it is also a humbling thing; and the man who has not been humbled in the presence of God will never be a worshiper of God at all. He may be a church member who keeps the rules and obeys the discipline, and who tithes and goes to conference, but he'll never be a worshiper unless he is deeply humbled. "A humbling but delightful sense of admiring awe." There's an awesomeness about God which is missing in our day altogether; there's little sense of admiring awe in the Church of Christ these days....

If there is no fear of God in our hearts, there can be no worship of God.

(A. W. Tozer, *Worship: The Missing Jewel of the Evangelical Church*, 8-9)

You may lose your dignity in your pursuit of His deity.

(*God's Favorite House*, 94)

Day	Date	Time	Location

Addicted to the Anointing

There is a big difference between encountering the anointing of God and encountering His glory. I'm not really interested in the anointing anymore—not when it is compared to the glory of His manifest presence. I say that because it is the only way I know to help people understand the dramatic difference between the anointing and the glory of God.

The anointing of God in all its various forms has a valid purpose in His plans and purposes. The problem is that we have become so addicted to the way the anointing makes us feel that we've turned our eyes and hearts away from the glory of God's face to get more of the anointing in His hands. The anointing empowers our flesh, and it makes us feel good. *That is why the Church is filled with "anointing junkies" on **both** sides of the pulpit*. Most (but not all) of the antics in our services that draw fire from the world and various segments of the Church can be traced to this odd addiction.

(*God's Favorite House*, 89-90)

The mark of a life anointed by the Spirit is that you know Christ in a living and ever-growing way.
(T. Austin-Sparks, from *An Open Heaven,*
in *The Refiner's Fire, vol. 1,* 10)

Day	Date	Time	Location

The Responsibility of Relationship

We would often rather be vicariously thrilled by God's touch on someone else's life than pursue it on our own. Or, if we are in the ministry, we can become addicted to people's infatuation with us because of the anointing. It feels so good to stand in the flow.

Addiction turns even the strongest anointing into a cheap thrill. At its worst, a preacher's uncontrollable craving to minister under the anointing—and a believer's driving compulsion to receive ministry under the anointing—becomes a form of "spiritual pornography." As in the physical variety of this compulsion, "spiritual pornographers" want to get their thrills by observing the intimacy experienced by *others* rather than shouldering the responsibility of *relationship* with God. This is the only proper channel through which we are to derive personal intimacy with God. The Lord doesn't want us to be infatuated with His hands and the blessings they bring to spirit, soul, and body. He wants us to fall head over heels in love with *Him!*

(*God's Favorite House*, 90-91)

We would often rather be vicariously thrilled by God's touch on someone else's life than pursue it on our own.

(*God's Favorite House*, 90)

GOD'S *Favorite* HOUSE JOURNAL

Day	Date	Time	Location

What's a Reputation Worth?

Does it shock you when I tell you that the world is tired of the "normal church"? It may be all that we have, but it hasn't done the job. I am not saying that we need to become a bunch of mindless fanatics, but the truth is that *our greatest temptation is the desire to maintain our composure at the cost of our convictions.*

We are not where we ought to be, and we are not doing what we ought to do. Why? *Because we think we have a reputation to maintain.* Reputations mean nothing to God. I am thinking of a King who made Himself of *no reputation* and took on the form of a servant just so He could do what He needed to do. *You can't seek His face and save yours. You may lose your dignity in your pursuit of His deity.*

Frankly, I've noticed that we need those unpredictable services that force us to lose our composure because that is often the only way we will allow God to break something open.

(*God's Favorite House*, 95)

The world doesn't fear Him because the Church doesn't fear Him.

(*God's Favorite House*, 67)

Day	Date	Time	Location

Love, Obedience, and Happiness

When the heart is devoted to God, we do not need to be perpetually reminded of our obligations to obey Him. They present themselves spontaneously and we fulfill them readily. We think not so much of the service as of the One served. The motivation which suggests the work inspires the pleasure....The performance is the gratification, and the omission is both a pain to the conscience and a wound to the affections....

"Thou shalt love the Lord thy God with all thy heart," (Deut. 6:5) is the primary law of our faith. Yet how apt are we to complain that we *cannot* love God, that we cannot maintain a devout relationship with Him! But would God, who is all justice, have commanded that of which He knew we were incapable?...This would be to charge omniscience with folly, and infinite goodness with injustice. No, when He made duty and happiness inseparable, He neither made our duty unmanageable, nor our happiness unattainable.

(Hannah More, *Religion of the Heart*, 73-74)

God is within reach of us all, but to lay hold of him it is necessary that our hearts should be attuned to him.

(Sadhu Sundar Singh, from *With and Without Christ*, quoted in *Sadhu Sundar Singh: A Biography*, 72)

Day	Date	Time	Location

The Main Thing Is Christ

God is actively courting our love, but we think that things get too messy the way they are. We want to sanitize revival until it can be offered to people in a simple, shrink-wrapped, mass-produced package that is nice and tidy. Unfortunately for man's pride, *some of the things that make God comfortable also tend to make men incredibly uncomfortable....*

Don't bother to look for shortcuts to revival or a revelation of God's glory. If you want to pursue God, then you will have to do it the same way they wooed and won, and chased and pursued Him in the past. *There is no new method or path to revival.* We just need to rediscover God's original recipe and quit dabbling. *We have majored on the minors* for so long that we have lost the pursuit of God Himself. Let me share with you some wise counsel my father gave me: *The main thing is to keep the main thing the main thing.* The main thing is Him, the centrality of Christ!

(God's Favorite House, 96-97)

I want Him. I long to see His glory and dwell in His manifest presence more than I long for the blessings of His hands.

(*God's Favorite House*, 99)

Day	Date	Time	Location

God's First Choice

If you are anointed, you will preach better, pray better, minister better, and worship better and with greater freedom, but that is not His highest purpose. *The anointing is all about us, but the glory is all about Him....*

The difference between the anointing of God and the glory of God is like the difference between the tiny blue spark of static electricity and the raw power of a 440-volt power line overhead or a lightning strike on your head!...The one will thrill you a little, but you get the feeling the other might kill you or change your life forever.

I love the anointing of God, and I am thankful for every good gift He has given us. Yet I am convinced God's first choice is for us to seek His face of favor rather than His hand of anointing....Personally, I've had enough anointed preaching and singing to last me two lifetimes. It's good and it's thrilling, but I must tell you the anointing in and of itself is not going to get the job done. *We must have the manifest presence of God Himself on display for the world.*

(*God's Favorite House*, 101-102)

Begin to practice the presence of God.
(A. W. Tozer, from *Man: The Dwelling Place of God*,
quoted in *Gems From Tozer*, 69)

Day	Date	Time	Location

The Priority of Heaven

If we're not careful, we can get so enmeshed in the machinery of "having church" and having a good time that we forget the purpose of worship. Our general opinion of worship is often expressed with the statement, "Well, I'm going to be a little late for church. I'll miss the worship, but I'll get there for the Word."

What we fail to realize is that as far as God is concerned, *worship is His part*, and *the Word is our part.* That means that if we miss the worship, we've missed His best part where we give to Him....

God doesn't get anything out of our preaching. *I am not saying that the preaching of God's Word isn't important.* I am saying that worship is more important to God than preaching because worship builds the basket or container for the fresh bread of Heaven. If you build a mercy seat, then you can have the glory of God come in, and worship is what builds the seat of God. Ask yourself this question: "What is the priority of Heaven?" To talk *to* Him or talk *about* Him?

(*God's Favorite House*, 106-107)

As far as God is concerned, **worship is His part,** and **the Word is our part.**

(*God's Favorite House*, 107)

Day	Date	Time	Location

Do You Want Him?

Wanting God! Wanting the fellowship of the Spirit! Wanting the walk with Him! Wanting communion with Him! Everything else is no good. You want the association with God, and God says, "I will come and walk with you. I will sup with you and you with Me, and I will live in you." A joyful hallelujah! We can attain to a spiritual majority, a fullness of Christ, a place where God becomes the perfect Father and the Holy Spirit has a rightful place as never before. The Holy Spirit breathes through us and says, "You are my Father, You are my Father." The Spirit cries, "Abba, Father, My Father." Oh, it is wonderful! And may God grant to us the richness of His pleasure, that unfolding of His will, that consciousness of His countenance upon us....

God is willing to bestow on us all things that pertain to life and godliness. Oh, it was the love of God that brought Jesus. And it is this same love that helps you and me to believe.

In every weakness God will be your strength. You who need His touch, remember that He loves you.

(Smith Wigglesworth, quoted in *Promises for Spirit-Led Living*, 53, 55)

_____

_____

_____

_____

_____

_____

_____

_____

_____

_____

_____

Worldliness is that which cools my affection toward God.

(Smith Wigglesworth, quoted in
Smith Wigglesworth: The Secret of His Power, 25)

Day	Date	Time	Location

Thirsty for Living Water

Can you picture Jesus leaning against a raised wall at Jacob's well, looking at the wristwatch of eternity and saying to Himself, "She should be coming any moment now." God the Son had an appointment with a woman of the world. *She had a blind date with destiny and didn't even know about it.*

Perhaps you can remember the day and time your destiny intercepted with deity—did you have any idea that you were about to have a God encounter? *That is because God set the appointment and you didn't....*

As this woman walked up to Jacob's well,...[Jesus] said, "I would like some water."...

"If you knew the gift of God, and who it is who says to you, 'Give me a drink,' you would have asked Him, and He would have given you living water" (Jn. 4:10 NKJV) ...

Jesus ultimately helped the woman understand that He wasn't talking about the kind of water found in Jacob's well. He was talking about living water and worship....

That Samaritan woman had walked to Jacob's well with a thirst for well water, but she wound up meeting the Well of Life and discovered she was really thirsty for living water. Jesus told her, "The Father is seeking such to worship Him." The *only thing that the Father is actively seeking is worshipers!*

(*God's Favorite House*, 108-110)

_____

_____

_____

_____

_____

_____

_____

As water is restless until it reaches its level, so the soul has not peace until it rests in God.

(Sadhu Sundar Singh, from *With and Without Christ*, quoted in *Sadhu Sundar Singh: A Biography*, 34)

Day	Date	Time	Location

Perfection or Presence?

Despite years of research, *I cannot find a single place in the Bible where music is mentioned as a part of Heaven's environment after the fall of satan....*

If music fell when satan fell, then that explains why the bulk of the satanic influence in our world comes from the realm of music. Music is his venue, so we shouldn't be surprised that the first place problems often show up in most churches is in the area of music and worship....

Our music may never be as good as the world's music because our value system is different from the world's. We are not after perfection so much as we are after Presence.

When the Church turns all its focus and energies toward the technical and professional perfection of our well-rehearsed music, our crafted sermons, and our tightly scripted services, we can unknowingly begin competing in the wrong arena. We need to stick with the one arena in which no one can compete with us—the art and ability to pull down the manifest presence of God. *Technical perfection may win the praise of men, but only the anointing and glory of God can melt their hardened hearts.*

(*God's Favorite House*, 111-112)

_____

_____

_____

_____

_____

_____

_____

_____

God is looking for a Bride-Church that has eyes only for Him.

(*God's Favorite House*, 102)

Day	Date	Time	Location

Worship Is Our Service

In the Old Testament service and worship were synonymous. "Let my people go, that they may serve me" (Ex. vii.16). That statement...was linked up with the demand that they took their cattle for sacrifices, that they might worship the Lord. Worship was the service, and...I am concerned...that we recast our whole idea and conception of Christian work or service. We have the idea that doing a lot of things in this way, that way, and another way, is the service of the Lord, and I want to say with strength and emphasis that all service to the Lord is determined, in its value, by how much more the Lord really gets of a place *for Himself* in spiritual reality, and not how many things we do, both in number and kind. The heart, the very core of service is worship; which means that God gets an enlarged place and Satan loses ground. Judge all service by that—not by the things done, but by the spiritual issue, that there is something more coming to the Lord.

(T. Austin Sparks, *The Ultimate Issue of the Universe*, 24-25)

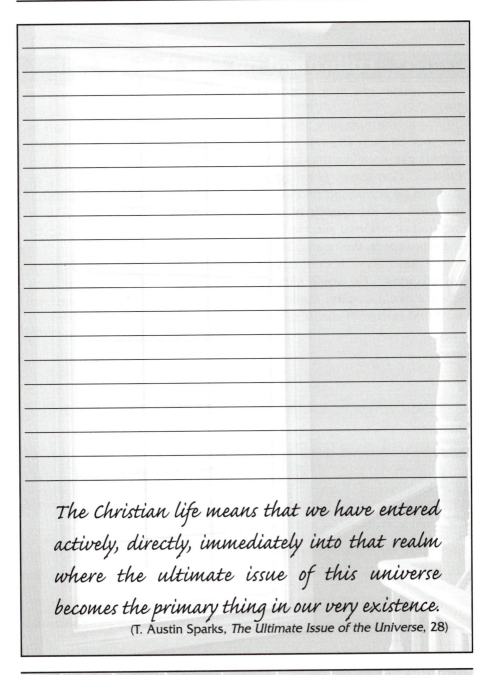

The Christian life means that we have entered actively, directly, immediately into that realm where the ultimate issue of this universe becomes the primary thing in our very existence.
(T. Austin Sparks, *The Ultimate Issue of the Universe*, 28)

Day	Date	Time	Location

Enthroned on Our Praise

Have you ever wondered why God is attracted to our pitiful praise?...

In the twinkling of an eye, the manifest presence of God is transported from Heaven to the middle of a huddle of prostrate worshipers gathered in a tear-stained circle singing, "Holy, holy, holy is the Lord...." *God leaves His magnificent throne of Heaven and comes to earth to be enthroned on the pitiful praises of His people....* God isn't attracted by the quality of our worship or our musical ability. *It is because of who we are.* He is attracted because of His relationship to the worshipers. We're His children!...

God says, "It's not how pretty they do it. It's just that they are My offspring." *He would rather hear you stumble through a song with a voice like a cracked foghorn than to hear the six-winged seraphim surround Him with chants of "holy" in tones of heavenly perfection.*

(*God's Favorite House*, 113, 115-116)

God is more committed to character than to talent.

(*God's Favorite House*, 92)

| Day | Date | Time | Location |

Song of the Heart

God is going to and fro in the earth right now, auditioning hearts to see who will become a true worshiper in His celestial choir. He isn't listening to the tonal quality of our voices or gauging our vocal ranges. Those things are unimportant to Him because His first concern is the song of the heart. Perhaps you are one of the many who are so desperate for an encounter with God that something inside you is pouring forth a passionate and hungry song of the heart. Can I tell you something? He is standing there right in front of you saying, "Keep singing. This is exactly what I've come for."

If you knew how close He is to you and how carefully He listens to every whispered amen and every crackle of your broken heart, you would be shocked. *The only thing the Father actively seeks is worshipers*...Don't worry, He has placed His ear to your heart to see if you can hit that note. Can you?

(*God's Favorite House*, 118)

_____
_____
_____
_____
_____
_____
_____
_____
_____
_____
_____
_____
_____
_____

You can't seek His face and save yours.

(God's Favorite House, 94)

Day	Date	Time	Location

Christ Alone Matters

The disciple...is called out, and has to forsake his old life in order that he may "exist" in the strictest sense of the word. The old life is left behind, and completely surrendered. The disciple is dragged out of his relative security into a life of absolute insecurity (that is, in truth, into the absolute security and safety of the fellowship of Jesus), from a life which is observable and calculable (it is, in fact, quite incalculable) into a life where everything is unobservable and fortuitous (that is, into one which is necessary and calculable), out of the realm of finite (which is in truth the infinite) into the realm of infinite possibilities (which is the one liberating reality). Again it is no universal law. Rather is it the exact opposite of all legality. It is nothing else than bondage to Jesus Christ alone, completely breaking through every programme, every ideal, every set of laws. No other significance is possible, since Jesus is the only significance. Beside Jesus nothing has any significance. He alone matters.

(Dietrich Bonhoeffer, *The Cost of Discipleship*, 62-63)

Nothing on earth, however sacred, must be allowed to come between Jesus and the man he has called—not even the law itself.

(Dietrich Bonhoeffer, *The Cost of Discipleship*, 65)

Day	Date	Time	Location

The Furnace of Desire

The soul must always have a heavenly vision to draw it out of itself, and away from the things of earth. The "eyes of the heart" must be illuminated to know the hope of its calling. The clearer the vision, the more entire the dependence upon the Holy Spirit for its fulfilment, and the more intense the thirst after God—a "furnace of intense desire" which must be created by the Eternal Spirit Himself, and which is the supreme condition for knowing God.

(Jessie Penn-Lewis, *Thy Hidden Ones*, 11)

"Father, we want an encounter with You that causes us to leave our waterpots at the well of man's religion. We want an encounter with You that we cannot get over. Turn our rejection into acceptance and our dusty, dry wells into inner spring experiences. We want to give You the best part—we give You worship and praise, adoration and thanksgiving in Jesus' name."

(*God's Favorite House*, 119)

If you want the fire of God—become the fuel of God!

(*God's Favorite House*, 132)

Day	Date	Time	Location

God-Sent Revival

Sometimes we have false premises about revival and the people God uses in true revivals....Someone asked Duncan Campbell to define revival, and he touched on this in his reply:...

"But in revival God moves in the region. Suddenly the community becomes God conscious, and the Spirit of God grips men and women in such a way that even work is given up as people give themselves to waiting upon God. In the midst of the Lewis Awakening [what we call the Hebrides revival], the parish minister...wrote, 'The Spirit of the Lord was resting wonderfully on the different townships of the region. His presence was in the homes of the people, on the meadow, and the moorland, and the public roads.'

"This presence of God is the supreme characteristic of a God-sent revival. Of the hundreds who found Jesus Christ during this time, fully 75 percent were saved before they came near a meeting, or heard a sermon by myself or any other minister in the parish. The power of God was moving in an operation that the fear of God gripped the souls of men before they ever reached the meetings."

(God's Favorite House, 123-124)

Duncan Campbell (1898-1972) was raised in the Highlands of Scotland. He came to the Lord as a teenager and served congregations of the United Free Church (Presbyterian) and as an itinerant evangelist. In addition to his involvement in the Lewis Awakening, he was much in demand as a speaker throughout the British Isles.

Duncan Campbell was so remarkably blessed and used by God in Scotland and many other places. In commending the study of his biography, Dr. Martyn Lloyd-Jones stated that, "in private conversation, as well as in his preaching, Duncan Campbell's emphasis was always on the Lordship and the power of the Holy Spirit." His chief desire was to see God powerfully at work in the lives of those around him and his whole life was devoted to that end.

Perhaps no one has influenced my hunger for the "Reviver" like Duncan Campbell. I have managed to collect several of his preaching tapes (available). His retelling of "When God Came Down," the Hebrides Revival, fuels the fires of my personal passion. The story of the two elderly sisters praying and worshiping prior to the outbreak of God illustrates what happens when you build God's Favorite House.

Day	Date	Time	Location

Worship Brings God's Presence

We need mass Damascus Road experiences, where the glory of God is revealed to an entire assembly of people all at once....Now picture the glory of God riveting entire communities with conviction after engulfing them in the light of His glory!

This is the way to win the lost. If worship is done right, then soul-winning and altar calls don't take a whole lot of words. Simply say, "Come," and they will. Why? Worship brings God's presence, and His presence drives away everything else. That means people in the *throne zone* may be given for the first time the opportunity of an unfettered choice when His presence comes.

The coming revival is not going to be about *sermons and information*; it's going to be about *worship and impartation*. The preaching of the Word won't stop, but the sermons that come will serve the same purpose as Peter's impromptu sermon on the Day of Pentecost. They won't necessarily *produce* desired actions in people; they will come after the fact to *explain* what happened after "God came down."

(*God's Favorite House*, 127-128)

A God-sent revival is always a revival of holiness.
(Duncan Campbell)

Day	Date	Time	Location

Do You Care About His Honor?

You have already seen what trials and afflictions these souls have suffered because of their desire to die and thus to enjoy Our Lord. They have now an equally strong desire to serve Him, and to sing His praise, and to help some soul if they can....Their conception of glory is of being able in some way to help the Crucified, especially when they see how often people offend Him and how few there are who really care about His honor and are detached from everything else....In short, the desires of these souls are no longer for consolations or favors, for they have with them the Lord Himself and it is His Majesty Who now lives in them....These souls have a marked detachment from everything and a desire to be always either alone or busy with something that is to some soul's advantage. They have no aridities or interior trials but a remembrance of Our Lord and a tender love for Him, so that they would like never to be doing anything but giving Him praise.

(Teresa of Ávila, *The Interior Castle*, http://www.ccel.org/t/teresa/castle/castle.html)

True faith. . . is a life-giving principle. It must be infused into the habit as well as enlightening the understanding.

(Hannah More, *Religion of the Heart*, 15)

| Day | Date | Time | Location |

The "Suddenly" of God

"Suddenly" there came an upper room experience where He threw open the windows of Heaven and rushed down. That's what we want: the rushing in of God, that suddenly of God. *But you don't have the "suddenly of God" without the "waiting of man."* We need to go after the face of God. We can no longer be content with God's just slipping His hand out from under the veil to dispense gospel goodies to us anymore. We want the veil to open, and we want to pass through into the Holy of Holies to have a life-changing encounter with Him. Then we need to prop open that veil with Davidic passion and worship so the glory of God will manifest itself in the streets of the city....

On the day the Church rises up to build a mercy seat according to the pattern of Heaven, God...will literally set up a throne zone in our midst! Let me assure you that when the glory of God shows up like that, we won't have to advertise or promote anything. Once the Bread of Heaven takes His seat among us, the hungry will come.

(*God's Favorite House*, 128-129)

Prayer is petitioning—"seeking His face" is positioning.

(*God's Favorite House,* 127)

Day	Date	Time	Location

Pursue God at Any Cost

There is one fail-safe way to open the gates of Heaven and close the gates of hell on the ruling principalities and powers of darkness in your region. Pray, repent, intercede, and worship God until you break open a hole in the heavens and God flips on His glory light switch. Satanic forces will flee in every direction!…

The status quo isn't working. We can't get the world into our church buildings—our lifestyles have convinced people that we don't have anything to offer them. We must get the "God of the Church" to them.

It is up to us. We can remain satisfied with our bland diets of powerless services interspersed with a few "good" services each year, or we can pursue God at any cost.…He is redefining the Church and making our religious labels totally obsolete. I can tell you this much about it: *His manifest presence is going to be supreme.* That means it won't really matter who speaks, who sings, who prays, or who does anything in those services—*as long as He is there.*

(*God's Favorite House*, 129-130)

_____

_____

_____

_____

_____

_____

_____

_____

_____

_____

_____

The primary purpose of the Church is to attract Him!

(*God's Favorite House*, 131)

Day	Date	Time	Location

Purity of Spirit

How rare it is these days to find a pure spirit. Usually whenever our spirit comes forth, so does our soul; they are fixed. So the first requirement in God's work is a pure, not a powerful spirit. Those who neglect this, though their work may be done in power, will find it destroyed due to the lack of purity. Though they may truly possess the power of God, yet because their spirit is mixed, they are destroying what they build....

One whose outward man has not been dealt with cannot expect the power that flows from within him to be pure....

Impurity is the biggest problem in the lives of God's servants. Frequently we touch both life and death in our brother. We find God but also self, a meek spirit but also stubbornness, the Holy Spirit but also the flesh—all in the same person....Thus, for God to use you as a minister of His Word, for you to be God's mouthpiece, you must seek God's favor by praying: "Oh God, do a work in me, to break, to divide, my outward man."

(Watchman Nee, *The Release of the Spirit*, 65-67)

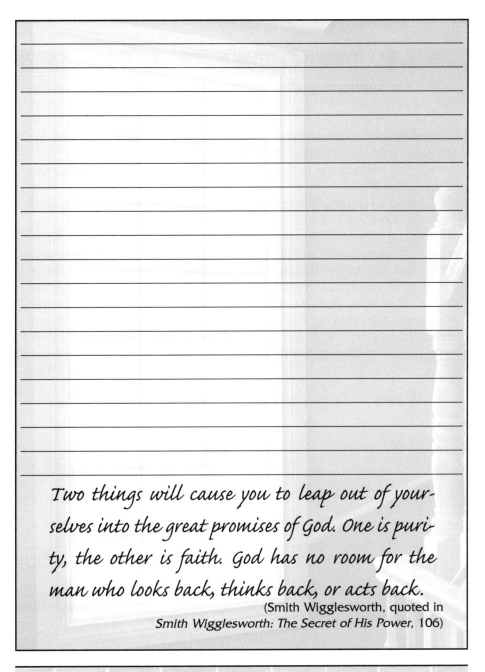

Two things will cause you to leap out of your-selves into the great promises of God. One is puri-ty, the other is faith. God has no room for the man who looks back, thinks back, or acts back.
(Smith Wigglesworth, quoted in
Smith Wigglesworth: The Secret of His Power, 106)

Day	Date	Time	Location

More of God, Less of Man

We must learn how to attract God to the Church in such a way that He can manifest His glory freely. When that happens, we won't have to worry about attracting men. God will do it Himself. "Presence" evangelism occurs when Jesus is lifted up in all His glory, because He promised that *He* will draw all men to Himself....

The bottom line is simply this: *We need more of God and less of man....*

You may be right at the door to the throne zone this very moment. God wants to meet you where you are. You can leave this divine appointment with an impartation from God that can bring revival to your church and city and bring the prodigals home in your family. But no one can do it for you. You must personally walk through that door of death called repentance. The glory of God is waiting just on the other side, but *only dead men can see His face.* Only beaten worshipers can build the mercy seat through their broken, purified, and repentant worship. It is just possible that you might be the "somebody" who will change the destiny of a nation.

(*God's Favorite House*, 131)

Flesh-death often produces future destiny.

(*God's Favorite House*, 85)

Day	Date	Time	Location

Only Broken Vessels Can Hold His Glory

We need God in our midst. If we build the mercy seat, He will come. If we want God to show up in our churches, He will only come through the cracks of our brokenness, not through the wholeness of our arrogance. *Only broken earthly vessels can hold the heavenly glory*. It doesn't make sense, but it is true.

I can't pray anything upon you except my hunger. I am hungry for God, and He promised us that He would meet that need: "Blessed are they which do hunger and thirst...for they shall be filled" (Mt. 5:6 KJV). The glory cannot come to a full vessel. We must cry out for more of Him and less of us. We must empty our cups of "self" before He can fill them up with Himself. It is the only way to open the heavens and release the glory of God over our cities.

(*God's Favorite House*, 133)

_____

_____

_____

_____

_____

_____

_____

_____

_____

_____

_____

_____

_____

_____

Let us never judge God's Word by our experience, for the Word of God is true whatever our experience may be.

(Jessie Penn-Lewis, *Dying to Live*, 8)

Day	Date	Time	Location

Union With Christ

Will you not now contemplate the blessedness of an avowed and eternal union with Jesus, and take upon yourself, through His grace, the responsibilities of an everlasting covenant, to be wholly His for time and for eternity?...

If you ever thus take Christ as the Bridegroom of your soul, the decisive hour must arrive for the consummation of that union. It has only been delayed for want of an entire acquiescence on your part. The Heavenly Bridegroom even *now* is waiting with glorious attendants from the upper world to hear your decision, to bring on the consummation, and to ratify and record on the pages of eternity the infinitely responsible act. He now presents the terms of the covenant, and invites you in His strength to lay hold upon it. Will you keep Him longer waiting, and subject yourself to the fearful probability of His taking a final departure? or will you signalize this eventful, solemn hour on the annals of eternity, as the specific period when you subscribed your name to a covenant which brought you under obligations never to be annulled, to a perpetual surrender of your being to Him?

(Phoebe Palmer, *Entire Devotion to God*, 70-72)

Faith only becomes faith in the act of obedience.
(Dietrich Bonhoeffer, *The Cost of Discipleship*, 69)

GOD'S *Favorite* HOUSE JOURNAL

Day	Date	Time	Location

Create a "Throne Zone"

Can you imagine what will happen if we empty ourselves and His manifest presence comes? What will happen when God's manifest presence settles over a church in a city? We must create a throne zone and expand the parameters of the manifest presence of God where His glory is made available to everyone without a veil, a wall, or a gate.

When there is no barrier between God and man, you will hear Him if He whispers. It won't take a hurricane-force wind of God to move you; rather it will be just the gentlest zephyr, the smallest breeze, the lightest whisper from His heart. If we can create such a place through our repentant "beaten" worship, God will come. David's tabernacle was His "favorite house" because of its unveiled worship of intimacy. It is this atmosphere of intimacy that creates a place of divine habitation—a "throne zone" on earth as in Heaven—God's favorite house.

Jesus, let Your glory flow, let it flow. We seek Your face

(God's Favorite House, 133-134)

_____

_____

_____

_____

_____

_____

_____

_____

_____

_____

_____

_____

_____

Seeker-friendly is fine, but Spirit-friendly is fire!
(*God's Favorite House*, 149)

Day	Date	Time	Location

Doorkeeper at Heaven's Gate

The glory of God is pent up in Heaven like floodwaters behind a dam, and God has openly declared His intention to flood the whole world with the knowledge of His glory. Most of the time we don't really know where the door is or how to go through the door once we stumble across it for the first time....

The thing God promised is going to happen, and a flood of God's glory is going to come. It is going to start somewhere with someone, but where? Who will find the ancient keys that jingled in the hands of God when He told Peter, "Here are the keys to the Kingdom. Whatever you open on earth will be opened in Heaven"? (see Mt. 16:19) Who will hear a knock at the other side and slip that ancient key into that door to open the gate of Heaven? Wherever it happens, whoever opens that door, the result will be an unstoppable, immeasurable flood of the glory of God. If the glory of God is going to cover the earth, it has to start somewhere. Why not here? Why not you?

(God's Favorite House, 139-140)

_____

_____

_____

_____

_____

_____

_____

_____

_____

_____

_____

_____

_____

A doorkeeper in the house of God is a doorkeeper at the gate of Heaven.

(*God's Favorite House*, 138-139)

Day	Date	Time	Location

Spiritual Perfection

According to the laws of Nature, it is necessary to grow gradually by stages in order to attain perfection. In this way alone can we make ourselves ready and fit for the destiny for which we have been created. Sudden or hurried progress leaves us weak and imperfect.... Slow and gradual progress, therefore, is necessary for perfection.

It is true that perfection can be attained only in a perfect environment. But before entering the perfect environment we have to pass through an imperfect environment, where we have to make effort and struggle. This struggle makes us strong and ready for the perfect environment, just as the silkworm's struggle in the cocoon enables it to emerge as a beautiful butterfly. When we reach the perfect state, we shall see how these things which seem to have hindered us have really helped us, though mysteriously, to reach perfection.

In man, there are seeds of countless qualities which cannot develop in this world because the means here are not conducive towards their growth and development towards perfection. In the world to come they will find the environment necessary for the attainment of perfection. But the growth must begin here.

(Sadhu Sundar Singh, *Reality and Religion*, quoted in *Sadhu Sundar Singh: A Biography*, 24)

The Word of God well understood and religiously obeyed is the shortest route to spiritual perfection.
(A. W. Tozer, from *Of God and Men*, quoted in *Gems From Tozer*, 66)

Day	Date	Time	Location

Consecrate Yourself to God

God never intended for us to use our favorite hymns or worship songs to mark our divine encounters or to hold open the gates of Heaven. A sermon won't do it; nor will a sparkling personality or a powerful healing ministry do it. God has a better idea. *Prop open that gate with your own life!*

(God's Favorite House, 141)

The Lord Jesus never restricted God in any way. For nearly two thousand years, God has been working in the Church towards the day when the Church will no longer restrict Him. As Christ fully manifests God, so shall it be with the Church. Step by step God is instructing and dealing with His children; again and again we sense His hand upon us. So shall it be until that day when the Church is indeed the full manifestation of God....If we expect the gospel to be fully recovered, we must thoroughly consecrate ourselves to God even like those in the early Church. For the gospel to be recovered, consecration must be recovered. Both must be thorough. May God have an outlet through us.

(Watchman Nee, The Release of the Spirit, 56)

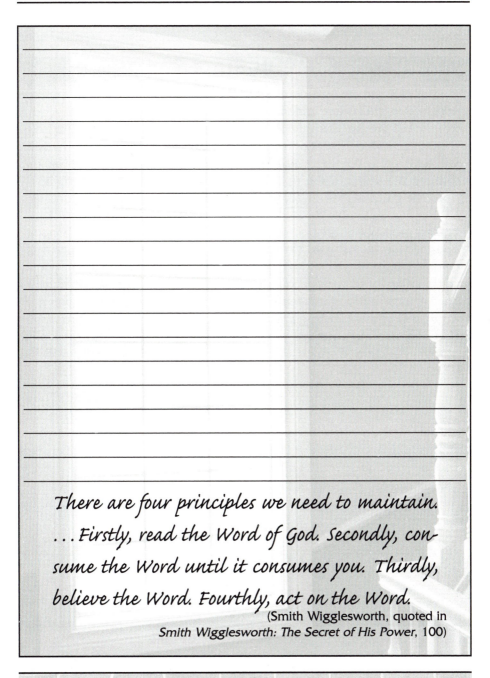

There are four principles we need to maintain. ...Firstly, read the Word of God. Secondly, consume the Word until it consumes you. Thirdly, believe the Word. Fourthly, act on the Word.

(Smith Wigglesworth, quoted in *Smith Wigglesworth: The Secret of His Power*, 100)

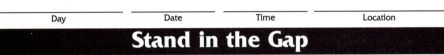

Day	Date	Time	Location

Stand in the Gap

Nothing beats a living, serving doorkeeper when it comes to ushering in guests and meeting needs.

Let me ask you this: *What is the purpose of the Church?* It isn't meant to serve only you or me. The Church is for Him above all. Now if we have an encounter with Him, if we somehow thrust our hands through the veil into the open heaven, it is our responsibility to hold open the gates of Heaven for the benefit of those who follow behind us.

If you stumble through that door in the midst of your repentant, beaten worship, then position yourself in the doorway and prop it open. *Stand in the gap.* God has promised He will help rebuild His favorite house, if we can hold the door open. If you can imagine your-self holding open a large overhead door with your hands, then you have a picture of a gatekeeper in the right place—*propping open the door to God's presence with upraised hands in the posture and posi-tion of praise and worship.*

(*God's Favorite House*, 141-142)

_____

_____

_____

_____

_____

_____

_____

_____

_____

_____

_____

_____

Live ready. *If you have to get ready when the opportunity comes your way, it will be too late. Opportunity does not wait, not even while you pray.*

(Smith Wigglesworth, quoted in
Smith Wigglesworth: The Secret of His Power, 111)

Day	Date	Time	Location

Famished for His Presence

The gradual disappearance of the idea and feeling of majesty from the Church is a sign and a portent. Our God has now become our servant to wait on our will. "The Lord is *my Shepherd*," we say, instead of "*The Lord* is my shepherd," and the difference is as wide as the world.

The Church has surrendered her once lofty concept of God and has substituted for it one so low, so ignoble, as to be utterly unworthy of thinking, worshipping men.

The low view of God entertained almost universally among Christians is the cause of a hundred lesser evils everywhere among us. A whole new philosophy of the Christian life has resulted from this one basic error in our religious thinking.

The world is perishing for lack of the knowledge of God and the Church is famishing for want of His Presence.

(A. W. Tozer, Gems From Tozer, 7)

The Church must no longer point toward repentance; we must lead the way with a lifestyle of repentance.

(*God's Favorite House*, 100)

Day	Date	Time	Location

The Most Influential Position in the World

When we open the windows of Heaven through our worship, we also need to post a guard—a doorkeeper—inside the dimension of God (worship) to hold open the windows of Heaven....

A gatekeeper can be anyone who has the responsibility of opening the windows of Heaven to a city. They could be church leaders, intercessors, and every worshiper. An open heaven refers to the free access of God's presence to man and to the free flow of God's glory to man's dimension, with as little demonic hindrance as possible....

David also was a gatekeeper, but he understood the importance of his office. When he penned Psalm 84:10, I feel that he was saying, "I would rather be a doorkeeper at the right door, because that is the place of *real* influence." *Never underestimate the power of God's presence.* If you can be a doorkeeper and open the door of the manifest presence of God to your church and your community, understand that you have been placed in the most influential position in the entire world.

(*God's Favorite House*, 142-143)

When you stand in the place of worship, you are literally opening up and swinging wide a spiritual gate, an entrance for the risen Lord.

(God's Favorite House, 146)

Day	Date	Time	Location

Our Unlimited Love

Everything which relates to God is infinite. We must therefore, while we keep our hearts humble, keep our aims high. Our highest services are indeed but finite, imperfect. But as God is unlimited in goodness, He should have our unlimited love. The best we can offer is poor, but let us not withhold that best. He deserves incomparably more than we have to give. Let us not give Him less than all. If He has ennobled our corrupt nature with spiritual desires, let us not refuse their noblest aspirations. Let Him not behold us so prodigally lavishing our affections on the smallest of His bounties that we have nothing left for Himself. As God's standard of everything is high, let us endeavor to live for Him with the highest intention of mind. Let us obey Him with the most intense love, adore Him with the most fervent gratitude. Let us "praise Him according to His excellent greatness." (Ps. 150:2) Let us serve Him with all the strength of our capacity, with all the devotion of our will.

(Hannah More, *Religion of the Heart*, 79-80)

When we are called to follow Christ, we are summoned to an exclusive attachment to his person.
(Dietrich Bonhoeffer, *The Cost of Discipleship*, 63)

Day	Date	Time	Location

Fear of Man Closes the Windows of Heaven

God is looking for people who have the keys to the Kingdom and know how to use them (that's you and me!). The sad part of it all is that not only can our obedient activity in praise and worship open Heaven and close hell, but *our inactivity can just as effectively open hell and close Heaven....*

Perhaps the greatest problem in the Church preventing the opening of the heavens today is the fear of man. It permeates pastoral leadership, and some leaders admit that the fear of man drives 90 percent of their decisions. *Man-oriented and man-pleasing decisions are driving the Church toward spiritual bankruptcy* and are closing the windows of Heaven. We must make up our minds that we are after only one thing: **We want God.** We want to open the windows of Heaven so His glory will flood our churches, our cities, and the lives of our people....

Are you willing to weep over your city like Jesus wept over Jerusalem?

(God's Favorite House, 148)

The Church is pregnant with God's purposes.

(*God's Favorite House*, 128)

Day	Date	Time	Location

An Open Heaven Is Our Birthright

By the coming of the Holy Spirit, the open heaven is made a reality. The Cross effects the opening of the heavens for us, but it is the Holy Spirit who makes it good in us, just as was the case in that typical or symbolic death and burial and resurrection of the Lord Jesus in Jordan when the heavens were opened to Him. Coming up on new, resurrection ground, He had the open heaven, the Spirit then alighted and abode upon Him, and the Spirit became, shall we say, the channel of communication, making the open heaven all that it should be as a matter of communication, intercourse, communion. It is the era of the Spirit making all the values of Christ real in us. That era has come. We are in the era of the Holy Spirit, of the open heaven.

[T]his open heaven...is for everyone....[O]ur very birthright is an open heaven. In other words, you and I may, in Christ, know this wonderful work of the Holy Spirit in an inward revelation of Christ in ever-growing fulness.

(T. Austin Sparks, quoted in *The Refiner's Fire*, 10-11)

If you get the door of Heaven propped open, don't ever let it close again!

(*God's Favorite House*, 136)

Day	Date	Time	Location

Prop Open the Windows of Heaven

You have the keys in your hand, transferred by the Spirit through the leadership of the Church since Jesus first delivered them into Peter's hands. Are you going to unlock the windows of Heaven and lock up the gates of hell? Will you prop open the door so the King of Glory can personally come in to *rebuild His favorite house,* **the house that worship built?**...

God is still hiding from the world because He cannot flow through the streets until the Church takes its place and begins to filter the glory. So the hunting eyes of God are darting to and fro while He asks, "Where is somebody who will be a go-between, who will stand in the gap and make up the hedge? Don't let it fall. Hold it high for other places and other people. I'm looking for somebody who can prop open the windows of Heaven in the weeping zone."

(God's Favorite House, 148-149)

With revelation comes responsibility.

(*God's Favorite House*, 149)

Day	Date	Time	Location

A Place of Habitation

Something is shaking the Church. We hit a bump, our new cart was shaken, and our Uzzahs are dying or dead. We want Him, but we've had to learn the right ways to welcome and reverence His presence. Our shaking hands have found the rip in the veil. We've found the door of Heaven, and God is looking for a place of habitation. Throw open the veil and keep it open....

Will the doorkeepers rise up and take their positions at the right door? Will the repentant, beaten worshipers turn their focus away from the bleating complaints of men to offer the sweet incense of praise to enthrone the Great King? If they do...if *we* do, *then He will come.* And He will build again the tabernacle of David, His house of unending, unveiled worship among redeemed men. Then the gates of Heaven will be opened and flood the Church, the cities, and the whole earth with the knowledge of His glory and draw all men unto Himself.

(God's Favorite House, 150)

When Christ calls a man, he bids him come and die.

(Dietrich Bonhoeffer, *The Cost of Discipleship*, 99)

GOD'S *Favorite* HOUSE JOURNAL

Bibliography

à Kempis, Thomas. *The Imitation of Christ.* <http://www.ccel.org/k/kempis/ imitation/imitation.htm>

Bonhoeffer, Dietrich. *The Cost of Discipleship.* New York: The Macmillan Company, 1963.

More, Hannah. *Religion of the Heart.* Orleans, MA: Paraclete Press, 1993.

Nee, Watchman. *The Release of the Spirit.* Cloverdale, IN: Sure Foundation, 1965.

Palmer, Phoebe. *Entire Devotion to God.* Salem, OH: Schmul Publishing Company, no copyright.

Penn-Lewis, Jessie. *Communion With God.* Parkstone Poole, Dorset, England: The Overcomer Literature Trust, no copyright.

—. *Dying to Live.* Parkstone Poole, Dorset, England: The Overcomer Literature Trust, no copyright.

—. *Face to Face.* Parkstone Poole, Dorset, England: The Overcomer Literature Trust, no copyright.

—. *Opened Heavens.* Dixon, MO: Rare Christian Books, no copyright.

—. *Thy Hidden Ones.* Parkstone Poole, Dorset, England: The Overcomer Literature Trust, no copyright.

Singh, Sadhu Sundar. *Reality and Religion,* as quoted in Thompson, Phyllis. *Sadhu Sundar Singh: A Biography of the Remarkable Indian Holy Man and Disciple of Jesus Christ.* Carlisle, Cumbria, CA: OM Publishing, 1992.

—. *With and Without Christ,* as quoted in Thompson, Phyllis. *Sadhu Sundar Singh: A Biography of the Remarkable Indian Holy Man*

and *Disciple of Jesus Christ*. Carlisle, Cumbria, CA: OM Publishing, 1992.

Sparks, T. Austin. *An Open Heaven*, as quoted in *The Refiner's Fire, vol. I.* Dixon, MO: Rare Christian Books, n.d.

—. *The Ultimate Issue of the Universe*. No copyright.

Tenney, Tommy. *God's Favorite House*. Shippensburg, PA: Destiny Image Publishers, 1999.

Teresa of Ávila. *The Interior Castle*, as quoted in Hazzard, David. *Majestic Is Your Name*. Minneapolis, MN: Bethany House Publishers, 1993.

—. *The Interior Castle*. <http://www.ccel.org/t/teresa/castle/castle.html>

Tozer, A.W. *Of God and Men*, as quoted in *Gems From Tozer*. Camp Hill, PA: Christian Publications, 1969.

—. *The Knowledge of the Holy*, as quoted in Tozer, *Gems From Tozer*. Camp Hill, PA: Christian Publications, 1969.

—. *Man: The Dwelling Place of God*, as quoted in *Gems From Tozer*. Camp Hill, PA: Christian Publications, 1969.

—. *That Incredible Christian*, as quoted in *Gems From Tozer*. Camp Hill, PA: Christian Publications, 1969.

—. *Tozer on Worship and Entertainment*. James L. Snyder, comp. Camp Hill, PA: Christian Publications, 1997.

—. *Whatever Happened to Worship?* Gerald B. Smith, ed. Camp Hill, PA: Christian Publications, 1985.

—. *Worship: The Missing Jewel in The Evangelical Church*. Camp Hill, PA: Christian Publications, n.d.

Wigglesworth, Smith. Quoted in *Promises for Spirit-Led Living*. Ann Arbor, MI: Servant Publications, 1999.

Wigglesworth, Smith. Quoted in Hibbert, Albert. *Smith Wigglesworth: The Secret of His Power*. Tulsa, OK: Harrison House, 1982.

GodChasers.network

GodChasers.network is the ministry of Tommy and Jeannie Tenney. Their heart's desire is to see the presence and power of God fall—not just in churches, but on cities and communities all over the world.

How to contact us:

By Mail:

> **GodChasers.network**
> **P.O. Box 3355**
> **Pineville, Louisiana 71361**
> **USA**

By Phone:

Voice:	318.44CHASE (318.442.4273)
Fax:	318.442.6884
Orders:	888.433.3355

By Internet:

E-mail:	Contact@GodChasers.net
Website:	www.GodChasers.net

Join Today

When you join the **GodChasers.network** we'll send you a free teaching tape!

If you share in our vision and want to stay current on how the Lord is using GodChasers.network, please add your name to our mailing list. We'd like to keep you updated on what the Spirit is saying through Tommy. We'll also send schedule updates and make you aware of new resources as they become available.

Sign up by calling or writing to (U.S. residents only):

Tommy Tenney
GodChasers.network
P.O. Box 3355
Pineville, Louisiana 71361-3355
USA

318-44CHASE (318.442.4273)
or sign up online at
http://www.GodChasers.net/lists/

We regret that we are only able to send regular postal mailings to US residents at this time. If you live outside the US you can still add your postal address to our mailing list—you will automatically begin to receive our mailings as soon as they are available in your area.

E-mail Announcement List

If you'd like to receive information from us via e-mail, join our E-mail Announcement List by visiting our web-site at www.GodChasers.net/lists/.

"Chase God" with us Online!

The **GodChasers.network** is proud to bring you some of the most family-friendly Internet access available today! We've partnered with some Internet leaders to provide state-of-the art facilities, national and international dialup coverage, and 24-hour technical support. This is truly the best that the Internet has to offer: a service that is both reliable and safe! We use the industry's ONLY true artificial intelligence filter, the BAIR™ filtering System, so you can surf the net in a wholesome environment!

Features:
- Exclusive GodChasers.network Content
- Email address: Yourname@GodChasers.net
- Chat channels with opportunities to talk with Tommy and Jeannie Tenney, GodChasers staff, and guests
- Artificial Intelligence text and picture filtering
- Full Internet Capabilities
- Instant messaging
- Streaming audio/video
- Download MP3 Music files
- Much Much More!

For more information or to sign up today, you can visit our web site at **http://www.GodChasers.com/**. You can also call or write to us to receive software by mail!

Run With Us!

Become a GodChasers.network Monthly Seed Partner

"Have you caught Him yet?"

We're asked a lot of questions like that— and with a name like "God-Chasers.network," we've come to expect it! Do we really think that we can "catch" God? Is God running away from us? What are we talking about?

"God chasers" are people whose hunger for Him compels them to run—not walk—towards a deeper and more meaningful relationship with the Almighty. For them, it isn't just a casual pursuit. Sundays and Wednesday nights aren't enough: they need Him every day, in every situation and circumstance, the good times and the bad.

Chasing God in our troubled times isn't always easy, but if we're really seeking God, and not just His blessings, then our cicumstances shouldn't hinder our pursuit. We will find God in trying times and learn that He is in control even when everything around us seems to be spinning out of control. He may *seem* distant from us...but when we pursue Him, we'll find that He *wants* us to "catch" Him, and He will draw near. That's what "chasing God" is all about!

Are you a "God chaser"? If the cries of your heart are echoed in the words of this message, would you prayerfully consider "running with us" as a GodChasers.network partner? Each month, our Seed Partners who sow into this ministry with a monthly gift of $20 or more receive a teaching tape. It's a small token of our gratitude, and helps our partners stay current with the direction and flow of the ministry.

Thank you for your interest in **GodChasers.network**. We look forward to chasing Him with you!

In Pursuit,

Tommy Tenney
& The GodChasers.network Staff

Become a Monthly Seed Partner
by calling or writing to:

Tommy Tenney
GodChasers.network
P.O. Box 3355
Pineville, Louisiana 71361-3355
318.44CHASE (318.442.4273)

AUDIOTAPE ALBUMS BY TOMMY TENNEY

FANNING THE FLAMES
(audiotape album) $20 plus $4.50 S&H

Tape 1 — The Application of the Blood and the Ark of the Covenant: Most of the churches in America today dwell in an outer-court experience. Jesus made atonement with His own blood, once for all, and the veil in the temple was rent from top to bottom.

Tape 2 — A Tale of Two Cities—Nazareth & Nineveh: Jesus spent more time in Nazareth than any other city, yet there was great resistance to the works of God there. In contrast, consider the characteristics of the people of Nineveh.

Tape 3 — The "I" Factor: Examine the difference between *ikabod* and *kabod* ("glory"). The arm of flesh cannot achieve what needs to be done. God doesn't need us; we need Him.

KEYS TO LIVING THE REVIVED LIFE
(audiotape album) $20 plus $4.50 S&H

Tape 1 - Fear Not: The principles that Tommy reveals teach us that to have no fear is to have faith, and that perfect love casts out fear, so we establish the trust of a child in our loving Father.

Tape 2 - Hanging in There: Have you ever been tempted to give up, quit, and throw in the towel? This message is a word of encouragement for you. Everybody has a place and a position in the Kingdom of God. Jeannie Tenney joins her husband and sings an inspiring chorus, "I'm Going Through."

Tape 3 - Fire of God: Fire purges the sewer of our souls and destroys the hidden things that would cause disease. Learn the way out of a repetitive cycle of seasonal times of failure.

NEW!
GOD'S DREAM TEAM AUDIO SERIES
(audiotape album) $20 plus $4.50 S&H

Only we can answer the only unanswered prayer of Jesus. "That they may be one!" This collection contains three of Tommy's messages on unity.

More titles
by Tommy Tenney

— **GOD'S FAVORITE HOUSE**

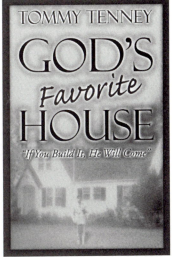

The burning desire of your heart can be fulfilled. God is looking for people just like you. He is a Lover in search of a people who will love Him in return. He is far more interested in you than He is interested in a building. He would hush all of Heaven's hosts to listen to your voice raised in heartfelt love songs to Him. This book will show you how to build a house of worship within, fulfilling your heart's desire and His!
ISBN 0-7684-2043-1

— **GOD CHASERS DAILY MEDITATION & PERSONAL JOURNAL**

Does your heart yearn to have an intimate relationship with your Lord? Perhaps you long to draw closer to your heavenly Father, but you don't know how or where to start. This *Daily Meditation & Personal Journal* will help you begin a journey that will change your life. As you read and journal, you'll find your spirit running to meet Him with a desire and fervor you've never before experienced. Let your heart hunger propel you into the chase of your life…after God!
ISBN 0-7684-2040-7

— **THE GOD CHASERS** (Best-selling **Destiny Image** book)
Also available in Spanish
ISBN 0-7899-0642-2

COMING SUMMER 2000
— **SECRET SOURCES OF POWER**
by T.F. Tenney with Tommy Tenney.
ISBN 0-7684-5000-4

Available at your local Christian bookstore.

Other books endorsed
by Tommy Tenney

━ DIGGING THE WELLS OF REVIVAL by Lou Engle

Foreword—Within our history lies our hope. *Digging the Wells of Revival* draws our attention to the spiritual inheritance of our country. From Azusa Street in Los Angeles at the turn of the century, to Toronto, Baltimore, and Brownsville as we face the next century, Lou Engle reminds us that what was, can be what is—where waters once flowed freely, they can again spring forth in this generation.
ISBN 0-7684-2015-6

━ A DIVINE CONFRONTATION by Graham Cooke

Foreword—If you choose to read this book, you should probably throw out your old ecclesiastical dictionary. Nothing is as it seems…it's bigger and better. Only we didn't know it! And Graham Cooke told us. Change is coming! The spiritual climate is about to be radically altered. Thank you, Graham, for "forthtelling" the spiritual weather patterns.
ISBN 0-7684-2039-3

━ THEY DRANK FROM THE RIVER AND DIED IN THE WILDERNESS by David Ravenhill

Foreword—Move from the place of *privilege* to the place of *purpose*, from the people of God *among* the nations, to the priests of God *to* the nations. The river is not the goal! It's a "gate"! Cross and enter—God's promises are in the promised land! Wildness is in the wilderness! The wilderness is only the *bridge* between slavery and sonship—Egypt and Canaan. Don't die en route!
ISBN 0-7684-2038-5

━ NO MORE SOUR GRAPES by Don Nori

Don Nori has masterfully passed on to us the lessons of true fatherhood. He states powerfully: "The children's deliverance is locked up in the parents' repentance." Amen, Father Don! I agree! I repent! *No more sour grapes!*
ISBN 0-7684-2037-7

━ THE LOST PASSIONS OF JESUS by Donald L. Milam, Jr.

This book is on fire! To be left unchanged you'd have to read it with asbestos gloves and an iceberg heart.
ISBN 0-9677402-0-7

Available at your local Christian bookstore.

Other books endorsed
by Tommy Tenney

— **FATHER, FORGIVE US!** by Jim W. Goll

This book is a road map to restoring the power and passion of forgiveness. How could we have neglected it so long? *Father, forgive us!*
ISBN 0-7684-2025-3

— **THE RELEASE OF THE HUMAN SPIRIT** by Frank Houston

The bindings on this book cover must be extra strong! That's the only thing I know that keeps this book from 'exploding'! Are you ready to release your spirit? To go to the next level?
ISBN 0-7684-2019-9

— **THE MARTYRS' TORCH** by Bruce Porter

The Body of Christ will be eternally grateful for what the pastor and parents of Rachel Scott share in this book. "There shall be light at evening time" (see Zech. 14:7b). We can see the future by the bright light of *The Martyrs' Torch*.
ISBN 0-7684-2046-6

— **THE RADICAL CHURCH** by Bryn Jones

He calls for a heavenly harmony where earth begins to sing on pitch with heaven's tune…where man prays the Lord's prayers instead of man's prayers. In Bryn's words, "Is it not time for passionate prophetic confrontation again?"
ISBN 0-7684-2022-9

— **POWER, HOLINESS, AND EVANGELISM** by Randy Clark

The future of the Church is at stake and this book has some answers. These authors speak eloquently, confirming what you have felt, affirming what you intuitively knew.
ISBN 1-56043-345-0

Available at your local Christian bookstore.

For more information and sample chapters, visit www.reapernet.com

6B-1:9

More
GOD CHASER
Products!

GOD CHASER HAT

GCH $17.99

GOD CHASER SHIRT

(M)	GCT-M	$16.99
(L)	GCT-L	$16.99
(XL)	GCT-XL	$16.99
(2X)	GCT-2XL	$18.99

**GOD CHASER
LICENSE PLATE**

GCLP $6.99

The Story Of Columbine

Excerpt from *The Martyrs' Torch:*
The Message of the Columbine Story

"I am not going to apologize for speaking the name of Jesus,
I am not going to justify my faith to them,
and I am not going to hide the light that God has put into
me. If I have to sacrifice everything... I will. I will take it."

Personal Journal Entry, Rachel Joy Scott, April 20, 1998

The blood of the martyrs is the seed of the church.

Tertullian

After her death, Rachel's family discovered her personal journals. They revealed a deep, secret relationship with Jesus that even her family knew little about. Rachel walked in a depth of relationship with Jesus that displayed a wisdom far beyond her years, and she actually seemed to foreshadow her death in several entries.

One of her personal journals was delayed in being returned to her family for several weeks after her death because it was in her backpack when she died. One of the bullets that passed through her small body was discovered inside her backpack and was considered police evidence until officially released. This bloodstained journal portion is breathtaking in ways you will soon discover.

Rachel surely loved her mother and father very much. Tragically, her family was all too typical of so many broken homes in our times. In her younger years, her dad was a pastor and her family a typical pastor's family. Sadly, in spite of such a nurturing, spiritual family structure, her mother and father tragically divorced more than ten years ago, when Rachel was a young child. After the divorce was final, Beth and Darrell had joint custody of the five children, Bethanee, Dana, Rachel, Craig, and Mike.

During those years Beth scrimped and saved, going to school at night while working during the day to support her children. Her son Craig once told me that he would sometimes hear her praying and crying in her bedroom late at night when times were especially hard.

A few days before Mother's Day, just weeks after Rachel's death, Beth was tenderly going through some of her daughter's many writings and drawings. From one of the stacks of papers, a page fell out into Beth's hands. There, in the beautiful script that only Rachel could write, and as a timely gift from a most loving heavenly Father, was the following poem:

SACRIFICE
should be her name,
because she has given up so much for us.

HUMBLE
should be her name,
because she will never admit the great things she has done.

FAITH
should be her name,
because she has enough to carry us, as well as herself,
through this crazy world.

STRENGTH
should be her name,
because she had enough to bear and take care of five children.

WISDOM
should be her name,
because her words and knowledge are worth more than gold.

BEAUTIFUL
should be her name,
because it is not only evident in her face,
but in her heart and soul as well.

GRACEFUL
should be her name,
because she carries herself as a true woman of God.

LOVING
should be her name,
because of the deepness of each hug and kiss she gives us.

ELIZABETH
is her name,
but I call her giving, humble, faithful,
strong, wise, beautiful, graceful, loving mom.

What mother does not yearn to hear such words of tender devotion from her daughter? Rachel has been described by her family as possessing a certain impish joy and uninhibited zeal for life. She would wear funny hats and took joy in wearing clothes that set the pace for fashion as she saw it. Her sisters told me that Rachel once put a message on the family phone recorder that said, "Hello, this is Princess Rachel. Which of her loyal subjects would you like to speak with?" Never at a loss for words, Rachel would say what she thought or felt, and she had a certain refreshing transparency toward everyone. She possessed a highly creative music talent. Her friends spoke of how she would sit at the piano and play the most beautiful music, enrapturing her listeners. When they begged her to play it again, she'd giggle and say she couldn't remember it because she had just made it up!

Once, while performing the mime presentation of "Watch the Lamb" to the music of Ray Boltz to her schoolmates at Columbine, the music suddenly stopped right in the middle of the performace. Well, Rachel just kept dancing! She went faithfully through the motions of her performance while several of her schoolmates chuckled. At last, when the music finally came on again, she was perfectly in sync with it! Everyone was amazed and moved by Rachel's tenacious determination. She won the respect of her classmates that night.

What was ironic about this incident is the fact that the young man who ran the sound system that evening was none other than Dylan Klebold. The music stopped in Rachel's life once, but she kept dancing. The second and final time the music stopped was when Rachel was killed. She is still dancing! No evil or power on earth can stop the heavenly music to which Rachel Joy Scott dances now.

Rachel's journals clearly reveal that she believed her time on earth would be brief. Her writings show a young woman fervent in her desire to serve God. Following is the last known entry in her dairy.

"Am I the only one who sees?
Am I the only one who craves Your glory?
Am I the only one who longs to be forever in Your loving arms?
All I want is for someone to walk with me through
these halls of a tragedy.
Please give me a loving friend who will carry Your name in the end.
Someone who longs to be with You.
Someone who will stay forever true."

At the Columbine Torchgrab Youth Rally, held in Littleton on August 7, Rachel's 16-year-old brother, Craig, said of his sister:…

The Martyrs' Torch
ISBN 0-7864-2046-6

Available at your local Christian bookstore.

For more information and sample chapters, visit www.reapernet.com

Exciting title

by Os Hillman

➤ TODAY GOD IS FIRST

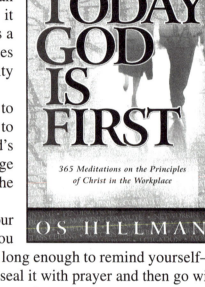

Yes, we all know that God is first every day, or at least He should be first. But can I be real for just a moment? Sometimes it is hard to keep Him first in my day. It is a struggle to see Him in the circumstances of my job. I need help to bring the reality of my Lord into my place of work.

Os Hillman has the uncanny ability to write just to my circumstance, exactly to my need. He helps me see from God's view. He strengthens my faith and courage to both see God and invite Him into the everyday trials and struggles of work.

So take this book to work, put it on your desk or table. Every day, just before you tackle the mountains before you, pause long enough to remind yourself—Today, God Is First. Read the devotion, seal it with prayer and then go win the day for yourself, your Lord and your work.

Excerpt from February 14

The disciples were traveling across the lake to Capernaum when a strong wind arose and the waters grew rough. Suddenly they saw a figure on the water, and they were terrified until Jesus called out to them and identified Himself.

Isn't that the first thing we do when unexpected calamities or even something that we have never experienced before comes into our life? We panic until we can see that God is behind these events in our lives.

ISBN 0-7684-2049-0

Available at your local Christian bookstore.

For more information and sample chapters, visit www.reapernet.com

6B-1:27

Devil Shrinking 101
The Classroom of the Spirit

Come with me now into the classroom of the Holy Spirit. The course of study includes a "workbook," a "laboratory" for experiments and yes, there will be a test! But do not make this a "crash course." Rather, take your time and learn how to rise above any and every opposing circumstance in your life. There will be difficult times of testing. You will be tried and proven, but there is genuine hope for success. Many students before you have graduated from this course with flying colors. One of the early graduates wrote:

> *For I am now ready to be offered, and the time of my departure is at hand. I have fought a good fight, I have finished my course, I have kept the faith: Henceforth there is laid up for me a crown of righteousness, which the Lord, the righteous judge, shall give me at that day: and not to me only, but unto all them also that love His appearing* (2 Timothy 4:6-8).

There will also be a diploma given upon the successful completion of your course of study. Each student will receive a plaque of recognition with the engraved words, "Well done, good and faithful servant" (Mt. 25:23). And the person handing out the diplomas and recognition will be the Creator of the universe, the King of kings and the Victor over death, hell, and the grave. He has been given all power in Heaven and earth. He is the man who carries the keys to hell. That's right, contrary to what some people believe, the devil does not even have the keys to his own house!

This little study guide, *Honey, I Shrunk the devil*, and the official textbook, the Holy Bible, can assist and equip you in completing your course of study. Other students in the class may discuss ideas and encourage you, but you will have to do your own work. To complete this class successfully you will need to work out your own deliverance. As a teacher's assistant, my goal for each student is simply "…that they may recover themselves out of the snare of the devil, who are taken captive by him at his will" (2 Tim. 2:26).

Before we begin our coursework, let's note that there are two primary facts about the world in which we live—there is a God and there is a devil. There is also one primary question each person will at some point answer: Who is bigger?

While there is no question who is actually greater in the universe and who will ultimately reign supreme, human perception varies from person to person. This perception determines to what degree a person will conquer and overcome his or her enemies. Some people see the devil as being too big for God to handle, let alone someone they themselves can conquer. For those who see or fear the "big monster," I offer a practical plan to shrink the devil. Together we can make him small enough to stomp! For those who have already discovered how to minimize the enemy, these pages will help to keep him small and not allow him to grow in their lives! Now, let's get down to business with some basic principles.

HONEY I SHRUNK THE DEVIL!
by Dianne Sloan
ISBN 0-7684-3026-7

Available at your local Christian bookstore.